Critical acclaim for Melvin Greer's

21st Century Leadership

Harnessing Innovation, Accelerating Business Success

"An outstanding thesis on leadership and the importance of innovation in the era of the new technology. Melvin Greer provides practical examples with scholarly references on what leaders need to know and do in our highly technical, social-media focused, human capital dependent global economy while highlighting the importance of fostering and managing innovation in this new environment. His book is a "Must Read" for every executive and manager for a roadmap for integrating leadership with current technological trends to create a successful organization. A "B-School" Masters-level course in a few, well-written pages!"

Art Chantker
President
Potomac Forum

"Again, Melvin Greer's theories on Leadership and Innovation challenge the status quo. He systematically chronicles the evolution of leadership and identifies unique and duplicative paradigms in innovative thought, as well as pinpoints strategies of next-level thinking in the magical processes required for successful leadership."

Kevin Manuel-Scott
Chairman and CEO
RONIN IT Services, LLC

"For the Greer Institute this book is a great accomplishment that not just technology leaders across the National Capital Region can use but a global tool that all leaders who run companies or government agencies can embrace to help guide them as they identify inflection points in their business where innovation can exponentially expand capacity and opportunity for citizen services."

Ken Tolson
Presidential Appointee
White House HBCU STEM and Innovation Committee

"This book is the answer to how we maintain economies, business and the leadership of business globally. Mr. Greer has masterfully defined for the world what it means to merge effective leadership with impactful disruptive innovation that not only provides new insight, but also really changes the way we live."

Rahman A. Parker
Chief Executive Officer
MAHN Healthcare

"Melvin Greer captures the essence of the latest and greatest in leadership; inspiring readers to grasp forward-thinking approaches and insights to accelerate personal growth".

Janelle Moore
Chief Executive Officer
Federal Concierge, LLC

"Mr. Greer's insights inspire leaders into taking control, drive new ways of thinking about disruptive innovation that take their companies to the next level. This book has the tools to redefine entire industries!

Sheyla Alfau Jimenez
Mechanical Engineer
University of Central Florida

"Melvin Greer unveils the freshest perspective on leadership paradigm shifts essential for meeting the business and workforce challenges of small and large businesses in his new work, "Leadership and Innovation: Harnessing the New Forces Used by Business to Succeed". Survivability is unlikely for those business leaders who fail to shift accordingly."

Rubin Cuffee
Co-Founder RuVal Enterprises

"Melvin Greer has answered the call of CEOs around the globe by offering a unique blend of theory and practice, both in leadership and business solutions, making it a refreshing read for decision makers with P&L responsibility."

John Gattasse
Aerospace Practice Leader
Appleby & Associates

Also by Melvin Greer

Software as a Service Inflection Point: Using Cloud Computing to Achieve Business Agility

The Web Services and Service Oriented Architecture Revolution: Using Web Services to deliver Business Value

21st Century Leadership

Harnessing Innovation,
Accelerating Business Success

By the author of *Software as a Service*
Inflection Point and *The Web Services and*
Service Oriented Architecture Revolution

Melvin B. Greer Jr.

iUniverse LLC
Bloomington

21st Century Leadership

Harnessing Innovation, Accelerating Business Success

iUniverse books may be ordered through booksellers or by contacting:

iUniverse
1663 Liberty Drive
Bloomington, IN 47403
www.iuniverse.com
1-800-Authors (1-800-288-4677)

ISBN: 978-1-4917-1674-8 (sc)
ISBN: 978-1-4917-1676-2 (hc)
ISBN: 978-1-4917-1675-5 (e)

Library of Congress Control Number: 2013921835

Printed in the United States of America.

iUniverse rev. date: 12/17/2013

For Stefan and Matteo

with

special thanks to my mom, Eleanor

As history has shown, no business model is safe from the results of an impactful technology.

—Melvin Greer

Contents

Foreword

Leading Innovation's Magic Is In the Turn, Not the Prestige

I recently attended a conference where the keynote was entitled "Innovation is Analogous to Magic". It reminded me of the opening dialogue of Christopher Nolan's 2006 film, The Prestige:

Every great magic trick consists of three parts or acts. The first part is called "The Pledge". The magician shows you something ordinary: a deck of cards, a bird or a man. He shows you this object. Perhaps he asks you to inspect it to see if it is indeed real, unaltered, and normal. But of course…it probably isn't. The second act is called "The Turn". The magician takes an ordinary object and makes it do something extraordinary. Now you're looking for the secret… but you won't find it, because of course you're not really looking. You don't really want to know. You want to be fooled. But you won't clap yet. Because making something disappear isn't enough; you have to bring it back. That's why every magic trick has a third act, the hardest part, the part we call "The Prestige.

It made me think that leading innovators take something ordinary, do some extraordinary things to it, and then make it re-appear in grandiose fashion. It's a great trick. It's so good, in fact, that I think it's fair to call it true magic. But modern leadership and innovation remains focused on The Turn, the process by which they make the ordinary extraordinary. Like a magic trick the leadership and innovation model I'm advocating also includes three parts, the adaptation of today's workforce and talent management, the enabling role of advanced technologies and the maturation of

STEM and STEAM into a leadership and innovation engine. But unlike many other innovators, I focus on all three parts.

While it lacks the pomp and circumstance of a prestige on stage at some big event, this leadership and innovation model is much more intimate, and as such, much more powerful. You may not perceive it directly, but the care and craft of The Turn percolates through your hands and eyes. Within minutes or even seconds, you just know this is something different. Something far beyond what others are doing with their false magic. You want this. You need this.

As an innovative leader are you focused on The Turn or The Prestige?

Preface

Melvin Greer, Senior Fellow, Chief Strategist Lockheed Martin and Managing Director, Greer Institute, has just released an amazing new book focused on maturing new leaders and inspiring future innovators. It's called "21ˢᵗ Century Leadership: Harnessing Innovation, Accelerating Business Success".

> "What an outstanding thesis on leadership and the importance of innovation in the era of the new technology. Melvin Greer provides practical examples with scholarly references on what leaders need to know and do in our highly technical, social-media focused, human capital dependent global economy while highlighting the importance of fostering and managing innovation in this new environment. His book is a "Must Read" for every executive and manager for a roadmap for integrating leadership with current technological trends to create a successful organization. This is A "B-School" Masters-level course in a few, well-written pages!" —Art Chantker, CEO Potomac Forum

Innovative leaders need to understand the behavioral, economic and social shifts that the new technology drivers are creating. Melvin translates these key fundamental shifts of workforce and talent management, disruptive innovation and creation of an innovation culture via STEM, into business impacts at the industry, organizational and individual level that ultimately drives a successful business strategy. Whether you are an executive, senior manger, millennial, teacher or student understanding the

21st Century Leadership and Innovation Model™ is critical for your success.

21st Century Leadership captures the essence of the latest and greatest in leadership, inspiring readers to grasp forward-thinking approaches and insights to accelerate personal growth.

Melvin Greer is Senior Fellow and Chief Strategist in the Lockheed Martin Chief Technology Office. With over twenty-five years of systems and software engineering experience, he is a recognized expert in service oriented architecture (SOA) and Cloud Computing. He functions as a principal investigator in advanced research studies. He significantly advances the body of knowledge in basic research and critical, highly advanced engineering and scientific disciplines. Mr. Greer has held numerous senior leadership positions, helping global enterprises based in Germany, U.K., and Brazil with their reengineering and transformational initiatives. He is the Founder and Chief Executive Officer of the Greer Institute for Leadership and Innovation, formed to apply Greer's research and to help find solutions to some of the most important global leadership and innovation challenges.

Mr. Greer has been awarded the BEYA 2012 Technologist of the Year Award, which recognizes his outstanding technical contribution and technical products that have a broad impact and high value to society as a whole. Melvin has been recognized for his outstanding technical contributions to cloud computing and service-oriented architecture. Mr. Greer is a Certified Enterprise Architect, Certified Gamification Designer, the Vice-chair of the Network Centric Operations Industry Consortium (NCOIC), Cloud Computing Working Group and an Advisory Council member of the Cloud Security Alliance.

In addition to his professional and investment roles, he is Fellow and Adjunct Faculty at the FEAC Institute and the University of Puerto Rico at Mayaguez, College of Engineering. He is also a member of the International Monetary Fund / World Bank,

Bretton Woods Committee. Mr. Greer is a frequent speaker at conferences and universities and is an accomplished author; "The Web Services and Service Oriented Architecture Revolution" and "Software as a Service Inflection Point, Using Cloud Computing to Achieve Business Agility" are his most recently published books.

Greer received his Bachelor of Science degree in Computer Information Systems and Technology and his Master of Science in Information Systems from American University, Wash. D.C. He also completed the Executive Leadership Program at the Cornell University, Johnson Graduate School.

Greer Institute for Leadership and Innovation

The Greer Institute for Leadership and Innovation is a nonprofit, nonpartisan think tank dedicated to improving the world through a modern perspective on the relationship between leadership and innovation. Founded on the theories of Senior Fellow and Chief Strategist Melvin Greer, the Institute offers a unique framework for understanding many of society's most pressing problems. Our mission is ambitious but clear: work to shape and elevate the conversation surrounding these issues through rigorous research and public outreach.

With an initial focus on workforce and talent adaptation, disruptive technologies and the maturation of STEM and STEAM, the Greer Institute is redefining the way policymakers, business and Government leaders, and innovators address the problems of our day by distilling and promoting the transformational power of modern leadership and innovation.

In 2005, Senior Fellow and Chief Strategist Melvin Greer authored his most recent book on the disruptive technologies associated with cloud computing. After working for nearly a year, Greer recognized that the book would be an initial foray into an ongoing conversation on leadership and innovation and that having a vehicle to conduct and promote ongoing research would be essential. As a result, in July of this year Mr. Greer founded the nonprofit think tank Greer Institute for Leadership and Innovation.

The Greer Institute is based in the Washington, D.C. Metropolitan Area.

21st Century Leadership

Harnessing Innovation,
Accelerating Business Success

Introduction

It is more important than ever for leaders to re-examine the current leadership models that take a fresh look at their contribution to innovation. Melvin Greer, Senior Fellow, Chief Strategist Lockheed Martin, is an advocate for a new leadership and innovation model where leaders can incorporate cutting edge innovative technologies, mature new leaders and inspire future innovators. Melvin will show you how to become an innovative leader in his new book "21st Century Leadership: Harnessing Innovation, Accelerating Business Success".

Traditionally Information Technology (IT) knowledge has been confined to the IT department, but not any more. In the same way any leader should be able to read a Profit & Loss or interpret and operate a balance sheet, they should be able to understand how technology will impact business strategy of the organization. A 21st Century leader needs to understand the behavioral, economic and social shift that the new technology drivers are creating, translate these key fundamental shifts of workforce and talent management, disruptive innovation and creation of a innovation culture via STEM, into business impacts at the industry, organizational and individual level and ultimately be able to devise a successful business strategy. Melvin's global experience illuminates what it takes to mature new leaders and inspire future innovators.

Webster's defines leadership as the office or position of a Leader; the capacity to lead; the act or an instance of leading. While the fundamental meaning of leadership has not changed much since the beginning of recorded history, this book will focus on the new 21st Century definitions of leadership and innovation. It will detail the key challenges that leaders face today including:

- Knowledge Driven Age
- Rapid Change
- Impactful Technology
- The new Consumer
- Organizations without boundaries
- Inter-Group Leadership
- Impact of Knowledge Workers

Leadership in the 21st century is no longer a fixed role. Today's leadership operates in a fluid, dynamic environment where innovation rules and leadership can come from any direction including outside the group.

I like to differentiate innovation from invention. While invention is the development of great ideas, innovation is the monetization of great ideas. Innovation is an important topic in the study of economics, business, entrepreneurship, design, technology, sociology, and engineering. While innovation is usually associated with the output of the process, this book will tend to focus on the process itself, from the origination of an idea to its transformation into something useful, to its implementation and its impact on the system within which the process of innovation unfolds.

Innovative leaders get out and proactively seek insight from their people about customer feedback, trend patterns and other critical organizational topics. They also have to allow a sense of autonomy within the ranks in order to encourage ownership of job responsibilities. This kind of autonomy allows for, among other benefits, a full-picture perspective of customer sentiment and loyalty to emerge.

The current leadership crisis requires an examination of 21st leadership and how innovation drives the continual evolution of what it means to be a leader.

Innovation Quiz

How up to speed are you on the innovative ways of companies and high-profile leaders present and past? Take this quiz and find out.

Q: Which food industry leader taps upon its employees to gain an uncanny and nearly telepathic edge on customer service?

A: Wegmans, the supermarket chain intensely trains workers to gauge customer needs while on the retail floor and provide input to management.

Q: Which entertainment giant is known for giving employees the freedom to manage their work?

A: Netflix, the company uses this technique to demonstrate respect for staffers' ability to self-direct and take ownership of their roles.

Q: Which company is legendary for its "walk-around" leadership style?

A: Marriott, Founder Bill Marriott always walked around his properties to connect with employees and ensure that hotels performed up to his standards.

Are you implementing any of these innovative approaches? What other innovative ways work for you?

Part 1:
Workforce Adaptation
Requires Modern Leadership

I suppose leadership at one time meant muscles;
but today it means getting along with people.
                                        —Mahatma Gandhi

Chapter One

A New Leadership Innovation Model

*There is nothing more difficult to take in
hand, more perilous to conduct, or more
uncertain in its success, than to take the lead
in the introduction of a new order of things.*
                                        —Niccolo Machiavelli

About 50 years ago, President John F. Kennedy presented the nation with a historic challenge: to land a man on the moon and return him safely to earth. That challenge was met within a decade. This bold challenge, coupled by the pressures of the cold war, ushered the United States into an area of unprecedented technological innovation to master the complexities of a manned moon landing and confirmed America's status as the world's industrial leader.

Everyone today comes in contact with the vast array of technologies and products spawned by innovations in the space program. These space inventions have helped to make our lives easier, safer, and more comfortable. Examples include research that led to the development of sunglasses that block damaging blue and ultraviolet light (Space technology spinoffs ultraviolet sunglasses) to imaging technologies that are the basis for all cell phone cameras and sophisticated medical HD (high definition) imaging devices (Space technology spinoffs cellphone camera)

Today's leaders need to challenge themselves to open new vistas of knowledge, spark innovation, and fuel economic growth. Although

3

the concept of leadership has been around for many centuries, in the 1930s, more significant studies began to attempt to define what allows an authentic leader to stand apart from the rest. Simply stated, a leadership model is literally a theory on how to influence and govern individuals toward the attainment of a goal. Numerous leadership models currently exist and some of the models that would have been adequate several years ago are no longer appropriate for these changing times. Looking at the global stage, there are signs of geopolitical and geo-economic shifts in the world order that can have a significant impact on leadership. It takes, vision, communications, collaboration and persuasion to deal with the new realities. Leaders need to be out of the box thinkers adept at collaboration, vision, strategy, and value creation. In order to compete in the new global economy, we need a new leadership model that was exemplified by President Kennedy that will help us prepare with the prerequisite skills needed to succeed.

Business Drivers

Business drivers are the resources, processes or conditions that are vital for the continued success and growth of a business and the achievement of business goals. Business drivers are also based on the type of products or services offered by the organization. A key business driver is something that has a major impact on the performance of your specific business. At a high level, the generally recognized key business drivers are the financials (e.g., cash flow & liquidity, profit), assets (e.g., equipment, facilities, inventory, and patents), growth, and people. Each driver is totally dependent on all of the other drivers.

Other business drivers can be either internal (e.g., strategies, goals) or external (e.g., regulations, weather factors, economic conditions) to a business. An example of a strategic business driver might be dealing with cyber threats on the organization. As the number of attacks and intrusions on organizations networks has grown exponentially, so has the cost of cyber-security and support staff.

A quandary is to create systems that are safe as well as usable especially with the many Bring Your Own Device (BYOD) mobile devices and applications that being brought onto the network. The cyber-security approach selected must be balanced between ease of installation and the ability to meet business and societal needs of the user community.

There will always be outside business drivers that a company cannot influence, but through good leadership, it will be prepared to handle them. A company must identify its business drivers and attempt to maximize the response to any that it can control. The rules of business have changed and demands leadership at the speed of thought and the capacity to establish decisive and inventive teams.

As American scientist, inventor, printer, philosopher, statesman, and businessman, Benjamin Franklin once stated, "Drive thy business or it will drive thee".

Every day, a business is exposed to risks and challenges that a leader must deal with. Constant change is a reality in today's business environment, and innovation and growth are two ways to handle it. Failure to adequately and timely respond to business drivers can put a company at a disadvantage. As organizations increase in size and scope, identifying business drivers becomes more difficult. Leaders have to look at these key drivers and need to know about generating cash as well as how to leverage it wisely to spur growth.

Although American industrialist Thomas J. Watson Sr. was not the founder of the Industrial Business Machines Corporation (IBM), he was the inspirational driving force that catapulted the company from a nondescript manufacturer of business equipment and furnishings to the world's dominant computer company. Upon becoming CEO of the Computing-Tabulating-Recording (CTR) Company, Watson's first act was to change the company name to IBM. He was known for his motivational and organization skills and posted the now famous slogan "Think" in company offices. While pursuing an aggressive research and development program, in 1937, Watson made the risky decision for the building of the Mark I – an Automatic Sequence Controlled Calculator, which gave the company the grounding and reputation as a leader in this new industry. According to Watson, "To be successful, you have to have your heart in your business, and your business in your heart."

Technology innovation is another key business driver and is one of the trends shaping the business world of tomorrow. Expect new business models to emerge based upon technology advances and the respective changes that will need to be made to organizational structures. Businesses *that fail to keep pace with these changes will lose their competitive edge.* The use of IT is leading the way with technology-led innovation. The four forces within Information Technology that are considered to be both innovative and disruptive are: Cloud Computing, Big Data, Social Media, and the Internet of Things. Technology disruption will continue and likely accelerate.

Consider some of the definitions of disruption:

- To throw into turmoil or disorder
- To interrupt the progress of
- To break or split (something) apart

With our fast paced society, disruption is happening at a faster rate and having far more impact. Disruption can be based on both Business and or Technologies. These new forces are destroying old business models and markets while creating new ones. Consider the new business models that have been formed through the digital inter-convergence of the traditional broadcasting and print media with the Internet or that of the financial services industry between banking and insurance. Do you believe that your business will not be disrupted within this decade?

The concept of "disruptive technology" refers to drastic innovations in current practices such that they have the potential to completely transform a currently existing area, as it currently exists — ultimately overtaking the incumbent technologies in the marketplace (Christensen, C, 2011). This term is sometimes used congruently with "disruptive innovation" which describes innovations that improve a product or service in ways that the market does not expect such as by designing for a different set of consumers in the new market.

Examples of this would include:
The innovation of the telephone disrupted the Western Union telegraph company when they did not see the significance of purchasing the patents to Alexander Graham Bell's telephone technology. Another more recent example being digital cameras has disrupted film-based cameras along with such iconic brands as Kodak. These are cases of new technologies replacing existing ones.

The same disruptive technological change can also be seen in alternative energy sources that replace oil, synthetic biology and gene therapies that advance medicine, and "smart" software and systems that automate routine jobs.

Other forms of disruptive innovation are based on existing technologies merging into new forms. Examples of this technical convergence include the cell phone, whose beginnings were for simple voice communications, and now evolving to a communications 'Swiss army knife' with voice and text communications, multimedia player, Internet browser, digital camera, and software applications platform.

Disruptive technologies may sometimes be difficult to recognize and may take a long time before they are significantly disruptive to established companies or organizations. Sometimes business leaders do not want to recognize that the light at the end of the tunnel is actually from the headlight of a train speeding toward them.

Disruption is something that keeps business and technology leaders up at night. Consider Risk of Innovation quadrant in Figure 1.

Ever business model comes inherent with their own risks. It is difficult to manage innovation and growth in a traditionally risk-averse climate. Safe incremental innovation hinders competitive opportunity. Incremental innovation is defined as "a series of small improvements to an existing product or product line that usually helps maintain or improve its competitive position over time. Incremental innovation is regularly used within the high technology business by companies that need to continue to improve their products to include new features increasingly desired by consumers". (incremental innovation, n.d.)

The core mentality of many organizations is the resistance to change. Maintaining status quo and sustaining your current business model may be the most cost effective in the short term but to the ultimate peril of the business. Organizations can expand their current base by leveraging what they already do well through the incorporation of new technologies or uses. In moving out of their comfort zones, many companies may not act prudently and take on more innovation risk than they can handle. Disruptive and transformational innovation occurs with breakthroughs or completely new offerings. Innovation is all about change that can be driven from many sources. Without true risk, there can be no innovation and with highest risk comes the highest reward.

These are forces that leaders face if they fail to adapt to strategic technological change as well as reach for leading edge opportunities. As the technology life cycle shortens, it requires rapid and decisive leadership to remain at the forefront of disruptive innovation.

An understanding of information technology is now considered a core competency among leadership. It is easy for leaders to make bad choices when lured with promising technology that could result in wasted time and money, all the while causing undue frustration to the organization. The foremost key business drivers of course are the staff and their related talents that drive the execution of critical decisions and constant innovation to move the business forward. Today, a working knowledge of computer hardware and software, a basic understanding of scientific and mathematical principles and the problem-solving skills are necessary for most good paying jobs.

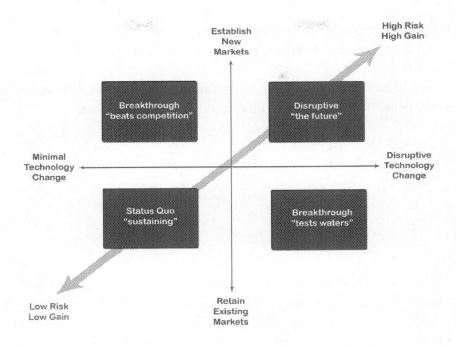

The Risk of Innovation

In the United States, there is a broad consensus that the long-term key to continued U.S. competitiveness in an increasingly global economic environment is the adequacy of supply and the quality of the workforce. While a whole range of internal and external factors affects the performance of every business, a good leader needs to focus on a handful of key drivers that:

- Reflect the performance and progress of your business.
- Are measurable.

- Can be compared to a standard
- Can be acted upon.

Turbulent change is the new norm in the business climate of the 21st century. Even though the book is dated, the concepts in Michael Porter' Competitive Strategy, remain strong. Leaders need to be constantly aware of the changing dynamics of potential competition that can be summarized in the five forces:

1. Threat of new entrants
2. Intensity of rivalry among existing competitors
3. Pressure from substitute products
4. Bargaining power of buyers
5. Bargaining power of suppliers

(Porter M. , 1998)

Today's cutting-edge innovations can become next week's technological white elephants. Gone are the days when a business could maintain a competitive advantage for a long period of time without changing their business strategy. Businesses that represent established technology may be the least likely to perceive the threat represented by radical innovation. Consider Kodak and its myopic focus on film.

Sometimes innovation is accidental by stumbling onto a solution to a problem that the business didn't realize that they had or a totally new approach to something. Although numerous accidental innovations exist, consider the most notable one that we probably use daily. The microwave oven was invented by accident by Raytheon engineer, Percy Spencer. While working on a radar research project, he was testing vacuum tubes known as magnetrons, when he noticed that a chocolate bar in his pocket had melted. Raytheon filed a patent in 1945 for the microwave oven and named it the Radarange. However, it was over twenty years later that Raytheon manufactured the first countertop microwave ovens, which forever changed how we cook.

Companies that can identify new and innovative opportunities for growth and rapidly adapt to new situations and rapidly capitalize on them will prosper. This needs to be a key business driver for 21st century organizations and leaders. This innovative spirit must be coupled by having a talented, imaginative, and experienced workforce that can drive the most innovative companies.

Innovation is not exclusive to only some of the large companies or brands that make up the FORTUNE list. Each year, FastCompany also ranks what it considers as the most innovative companies. (The world's 50 most innovative companies, 2013) While some of the companies are the same, FastCompany looks across the board at many smaller companies and some of the innovation that they have brought to the table. Looking at a portion of the list:

#5 Square cuts through the complexities of the credit card payments industry. For small businesses that are too small to justify the monthly fees and confusing rules and rates of a traditional credit card swipe machine, Square provides a tiny swipe reader that plugs into the headphone jack of an iPhone or iPad. Square mails this free device to anyone who requests it and collects a flat 2.75-percent fee from all transactions.

#9 Life Technologies is a global biotechnology tools company dedicated to improving the human condition. An example of this is its innovative system for speeding up genetic sequencing that showed its value during the latest flu outbreak. This $3.6 billion company has introduced 2,000 products since 2009.

#10 Solar City – According to SolarCity CEO Lyndon Rive, "of the more than 5,000 solar companies in the U.S., many of these companies will go out of business." But last year, while high visibility companies like Solyndra went bankrupt, SolarCity expanded and added 12,000 projects, all without a dollar of government funding. The key was being in tune with customers that are not familiar with the technology. Rather than just make the panels, Solar City is a full-service operation--designing, installing, financing, and maintaining every system.

#13 Tesla Motors is an innovative car company that emerged from nowhere. Consumer Reports is calling the Tesla Model S the best car it has ever tested. The Model S, an all-electric plug-in car, earned a score of 99 out of a possible 100 in the magazine's tests and was also named Motor Trends 2013 Car of the Year.

#26 – Legal Zoom makes a law firms' most lucrative work wills, uncontested divorces, and incorporations easily available by simply filling out a few on-line forms. Its new offering is online consulting that further disrupts the $200 billion legal market

#30 LinkedIn for continued new initiatives in the transformation of the professional career network into a must-visit hub of professional information sharing, even when people are not looking for their next job.

#38 UPS for listening to the customer and making missed deliveries a thing of the past by giving consumers a day's notice on a package's impending arrival with its free My Choice service.

#40 Chobani Greek-style yogurt has significantly muscled in on its larger, well-established powerhouse competitors (Dannon, and Yoplait) in less than five years from its inception. Entrepreneur founder and CEO Hamdi Ulukaya, a Turkish immigrant, entered the food business when he bought an old Kraft dairy plant that was being shuttered and the rest is history. He credits his success to "not knowing the old way of doing business."

Can you find some of the common denominators?

Change is coming

Steven Van Belleghem, one of Europe's thought leaders in the field of social media, conversations and digital marketing, believes that companies need to get ready for a new form of marketing to deal with the new breed of consumer. The new Consumer is smarter, more empowered, more demanding than any other previous generation and is redefining the marketplace. Technology is transforming their interactions with and expectations through the use of on-line tools and social media. Through social media, opinions are not only shared with friends, but on a larger scale. This form of communication can negate paid advertising or established good-will that an organization has. Now positive or negative experiences can be shared and passed on numerous times via tools like Facebook. How many Facebook friends or Twitter followers do you have?

Change is a significant business driver that all leaders need to contend with and is consistent across all businesses. In his Getting Ready for Marketing 2020 presentation, he identifies the areas of Extreme Customer Centricity, Technology as a Facilitator, and Selling without Selling as this new form of marketing.

Extreme Customer Centricity

In today's highly competitive global marketplace, regardless of your business area, strongly connecting with your customers is the key to success and long-term growth. Leaders must embrace business models that are customer-centric that encourage connection and collaboration. Customer collaboration is an essential component in innovation.

Peter Morton of IBM characterized the following five strategies to leverage a customer-centric approach across their organizations. (Morton, 2013)

1. **Drive flawless customer service across all interactions** by anticipating their behavior, then taking targeted action to keep them loyal.

2. **Anticipate and deliver in a social and mobile environment,** so your customers can buy, exchange information, and collaborate in the ways and channels that they prefer.

3. **Apply deep insights and take action in real-time** by gathering information and understanding customer behavior—both offline and online—in order to deliver timely and personalized interactions.

4. **Optimize sourcing and merchandizing based on customer demand,** to deliver the perfect order and drive top-line growth.

5. **Integrate and extend core processes and systems** to synchronize your value chain and take advantage of the investments you already have in place.

Further elaborating on these strategies: Customers should be excited in doing business with you and connected with you on a more personal basis. There are many stages of a customer' interaction with your company (i.e., discover, assess, purchase, receive, use, require support). These interactions must be examined and understood to create what has been deemed the overall Customer Experience (CX), which is the sum of all experiences a customer has with a supplier of goods and services. With the rapid growth of social media and mobile technologies, companies must adopt new approaches to interact with their customers. Opportunities now exist for companies to collect data from user interactions and from social media to gain new insights about their customers. This data helps create customer intelligence from the mountains of disconnected customer data the company collects on a daily basis to offer a big picture view. The voice of the consumer carries weight and influence, which is self-evident in the age of social media.

Businesses must understand the difference between customer loyalty and satisfaction. Customer loyalty is fragile and like any other relationship takes hard work to maintain and grow. If loyalty is based on price and convenience it becomes even more so. Despite the good reputation that it had with its customer base, online move rental/ streaming video company Netflix learned the hard way about the fragility of customer loyalty. It had taken on competitive Blockbuster video based on its ease of use and good customer communication. But when Netflix announced a new pricing structure, they were not transparent in their communications resulting in both a loss in customers and a drop in the value of the stock price. Customers also used social media as a forum to complain. (Evangelista, 2011)

Today's organization needs to focus on the customer and how to appropriately leverage the technologies to optimize customer engagement. "The goal as a company is to have customer service that is not just the best but legendary". - Sam Walton (1918-1992), legendary founder of Wal-Mart.

According to his book, *The Loyalty Leap*, author Bryan Pearson states that "Companies must not mistake one for the other. If customer satisfaction is viewed as true loyalty, then the company tricks itself into believing all is well and right between it and its customers. The scary truth, however, is that many satisfied customers are simply tolerating a company's services until they can find a competitor that offers a better price, service or location". (Pearson, 2012)

A case in point is Apple, where customer experience is the central theme. With their marketing strategy, they have created strong brand loyalty and have succeeded in making Apple products inspirational. They focus on their corporate stores where prospects receive undivided attention that includes personalized product setup upon purchase. Through Apple exercising control over the sales process, the staff is trained not to sell but rather provide solutions to customer's "pain points." Apple has expanded on its central theme by offering a harmonized, synchronized, and integrated user experience across all of its primary devices (iPad, iPhone, and Mac), using iCloud as the hub.

Technology as a Facilitator

General Electric is utilizing data visualization to realize benefits from social media data that gathers and analyses data in real time from many sources. In a specific case, they are using this Business Intelligence to help electric utilities identify and locate power outages through their Grid IQ Insight software. According to the Electric Research Power Institute, those outages and related disturbances cost utilities and consumers in the U.S. more than $150 billion annually.

"Today, utilities by and large rely on customer calls to find power outages," said Jonathan Garrity, product manager at GE Digital Energy. "We can interface with Twitter to complement customers calling in. For example, we can identify all tweets from a given geographic area that have key phrases like 'power outage.'" (General Electric to realize benefits from social media data visualization software, 2013) GE plans to roll out nine different Internet product platforms across their other business segments.

Since in 1995, Amazon.com has steadily grown from a "dot-com" corporation into a multinational domain of Internet retail. Amazon.com's vision "is to be earth's most customer centric company; to build a place where people can come to find and discover anything they might want to buy online." Originally focusing on selling books, some had predicted that the fledgling online bookseller would soon be crushed by Barnes & Noble (B&N), a book-retailing giant which had just launched its own site. Amazon's strategy of low product and shipping prices combined with a superior customer experience are the major underpinning in their success. Through its advanced IT infrastructure, it utilizes automated intelligent agents or "bots" continuously surf the web looking for competing prices to ensure that their customer gets the lowest price. Online shoppers are accustomed to comparing prices across the Web, but they may not realize that e-commerce sites, such as Amazon, also change their prices periodically over the course of a week.

Selling without Selling

The concept of Selling without Selling, which is otherwise known as Content Marketing, is the art of communicating with your customers and prospects without directly selling them a product or service. It is defined as "a marketing technique of creating and distributing relevant and valuable content to attract, acquire, and engage a clearly defined and understood target audience – with the objective of driving profitable customer action". (What is Content Marketing?) The goal is to deliver information that educates or entertains your target market in order to build up goodwill toward your brand that will ultimately be rewarded with their business and loyalty.

GE has long been known as a respected innovator and has mastered Content Marketing. Through the creation of the "Healthymagination" and "Ecomagination" marketing campaigns, they have aligned themselves with two movements that are widely supported - improved healthcare and environmentally responsible energy production. This is complemented with their "Imagination at Work" advertising campaign. Through these messages, they have established sites where people go to look for information.

In 2012, GE Healthcare has launched a new global awareness campaign that uses gamification and the power of collective wisdom propelled by social media to promote cancer prevention through healthier lifestyles. The goal was to encourage people to share their own health and fitness activities and what they are doing to help reduce their likelihood of developing cancer. During a six-week challenge, participants competed against one another while accumulating 'healthy' points and badges with the potential of being crowned Get Fit champions.

According to John Dineen, President and CEO, GE Healthcare, "Prevention and active participation in our own better health are the first steps in improving health outcomes. Leveraging the power of gaming and social networks to encourage lifestyles that can help prevent cancer isn't just a good idea – it's part of our original

Healthymagination commitment to bring actionable health content to consumers and our employees". (GE Healthcare Launches Social Media Driven Cancer Awareness and Prevention Campaign , 2012)

One component to Content Management is drawing the customer to your site. One potential approach is through the use of Gamification. This new gamer generation expects fast-paced action and continuous incremental reinforcement. To capture their attention, either as users or employees, gamification is required. While the word gamification has only recently emerged, the underlying concepts are based on Human Computer Interaction (HCI). Gamification is the process of taking the engagement mechanisms and tactics we find in games and incorporating them into ordinary activities to provoke a deeper user experience, engagement and dedication. People that are entering the workforce have been raised with computerized games as a form of entertainment. Note that applying gamification to an application does not result in a game. The intent is for users not to realize that they are playing a game.

As gamification extends beyond basic incentives and rewards programs through its utilization of Big Data generated by your customers as they constantly interact online, combining it with an understanding of human motivation, and using the data-driven motivational techniques of gamification, you can motivate, engage and create true loyalty.

Globalization and Workforce Diversity

Unlike never before, social forces are shaping the work environment, that includes workforce diversity, changing employee expectations, an aging workforce, and dealing with a boundary less global environment. The congruence of globalization, diversity and technology in the workplace encompasses a number of factors, ranging from familiarity with technology solutions to age and generation to gender to socioeconomic status and income.

A globalized world needs new leadership skills due to new challenges that differ from a bounded world to one that has become much more interconnected. The very word "global" intrinsically also connotes diversity which itself offers numerous challenges.

Globalization is the movement toward an interconnected world through integrated communications, culture, economics, finances, information, policies, politics, production, R&D, and trade that has become a business imperative for survival and growth. Globalization has resulted in opening of economies, global competition and interdependency of business. Business today gets done in a global marketplace. Globalization makes the economy of one country dependent on the economy of the other country. Any change in economy one country will affect the other. As a result of having a much more connected economy, we need a much more connected workforce.

Advances in technology have been a major player in advancing globalization. Improvements in telecommunications and transportation have increased both the efficiency of how people and things communicate and move. It's only in the last 150 years that advanced electrical signals could be sent over longer distances with the invention of the electrical telegraph that ultimately permitted people and commerce to almost instantly transmit messages across both continents and oceans, with widespread social and economic impacts. Further technological advancements such as the telephone, radio and television, satellite and fiber optic communications continued improving on the ability for people to communicate more easily and on a more cost-effective global basis. Cornell University, INSEAD and the United Nations - World Intellectual Property Organization (WIPO) co-publish The Global Innovation Index (GII), (global innovation index, 2013), which highlights the global nature of innovation and the increasing competitiveness of nations. Can you guess which country was ranked first?

With the continued proliferation of the Internet, e-commerce, and social media, many new leadership challenges and opportunities are rapidly evolving on all fronts. It's been less than 25 years since Tim Berners-Lee and Robert Cailliau introduced a prototype system that later became known as the World Wide Web (WWW). The Internet is simply a product of the technological revolution that started in the middle of the last century. Before that, we had the industrial revolution that was itself preceded by a social revolution, when people populated and formed the urban areas.

The concept of friction of distance is based on the notion that distance usually requires some amount of effort, money, and/or energy to overcome. As the "friction of distance" is lessened, the world begins to metaphorically shrink. Globalization also opens up the field of telework, alternative workplace strategies, and workplace flexibility. That said, the availability of the Internet and computer technology does vary according to socioeconomic status, which creates what's referred to as the digital divide, which separates the haves from the have-nots.

Advances in transportation technology allows for people to move about the world in search of a new job opportunity or a new home in order to improve their lives. Many migrations occur because lower standards of living and lower wages push individuals to places with a greater chance for economic success.

Developing countries are a popular place for investors to place their capital because of the enormous room for growth. The movement of capital can result in the expanding production or operations can often result in new job positions being created. Capital (money) can be moved globally with the ease of Electronic Funds Transfers (EFT) and a rise in perceived investment opportunities.

Operating globally opens up the business to new sources of cheaper labor, which results in existing employees losing jobs due to outsourcing. A prime example of this has been establishment of customer service call centers.

Today's labor pool is dramatically different than in the past. Greater income disparities are seen due to increased globalization and technology. Technology often leads to fewer lower skilled blue-collar jobs or production workers because machines and automated procedures are able to replace employees at a fraction of the cost. A brain drain is the migration of skilled workers from poorer countries to richer countries. Those that are more educated and have the skills and background to be competitive in the global marketplace will potentially earn higher wages. Generally brain drain results in poorer and developing countries lose of potential income that could be gained if these workers remained in their own country. No company can afford to unnecessarily restrict its ability to attract and retain the most talented employees available.

Science and technology are becoming ubiquitous features of many developing countries, as they integrate into the global economy. The ease of communications and economic globalization and partnerships between multinational organizations has made science a more global affair.

Globalization goes beyond just providing the option of operating in different countries and diverse markets. Global corporations not only sell products and services on a worldwide basis, they may also manufacture products and the underlying components in a number of different countries.

Multiculturalism

We all live and work in a multicultural world. In the 21st century, workforce diversity has become an essential business concern. People now represent workplace talent from a vast array of backgrounds and life experiences. Leaders have to judiciously adjust actions and policies to take into account such factors as culture, ethnicity, gender, language, and physical ability to the management puzzle. Competitive companies cannot allow discriminatory preferences and practices to impede them from attracting the best available talent within that pool.

To ensure that their products and services are designed to appeal to the ever-diversifying customer base, companies need to hire people, from all walks of life for their specialized regional or cultural knowledge and insight. This is especially true for companies that have direct interactions with the public, as the makeup of their workforce should reflect the makeup of their customer base. Diversity leads to creative solutions through the application of diverse heuristics, insights and perspectives that may not be available in a single homogeneous group of individuals.

The world's increasing globalization requires more interaction among people from diverse cultures, beliefs, and backgrounds than ever before. People no longer live and work in an inward-looking marketplace. People are now part of a worldwide economy and no longer live and work in an insular marketplace. Maximizing and capitalizing on workplace diversity has become an important issue for management today.

Diversity is generally defined as acknowledging, understanding, accepting, valuing, and celebrating differences among people with respect to age, class, ethnicity, gender, physical and mental ability, race, sexual orientation, spiritual practice, and public assistance status. (Esty, 1997)

Workforce Diversity refers to policies and practices that seek to include people within a workforce who are considered to be, in some way, different from those in the prevailing constituency. In addition to their job-specific abilities, employees are increasingly valued for the unique qualities and perspectives that they can also offer to the business. The emergence of diversity in organizations can be traced to the 1960s when legislation was enacted in the United States to prohibit discrimination against race, ethnicity, gender, religion, and national origin.

Diversity in the workplace can reduce lawsuits and increase marketing opportunities, recruitment, creativity, and business image. Negative attitudes and behaviors can be barriers to organizational diversity because they can harm working relationships and damage morale and work productivity. (Esty, 1997)

Managing diversity requires leadership skills need in a multi-cultural work environment. It involves recognizing the value of differences, presenting effective strategies, combating discrimination, and promoting inclusiveness.

The reduction in the friction of distance increases awareness and opportunity for the workforce.

"Diversity was the right thing to do in 1967, but in 2013 it's the sophisticated business thing to do," according to Shirley Engelmeier, the author of Inclusion: The New Business Advantage. There are many reasons why it is important to look at the broader business benefits of inclusion and diversity. She states that making inclusion part of a company's business strategy "helps to drive employee engagement, productivity, innovation and retention." (Engelmeier, 2012)

There is the possibility that the leadership and managerial skills within an organization that are practiced today might not be feasible in a global scale. Globalization and diversity complicate the process that the diverse environments and cultures must be taken into account.

Researchers conducted studies at MIT's Center for Collective Intelligence and Carnegie Mellon, MIT and Carnegie Mellon, (CMU Collective Intelligence Study, 2010) that showed that when it comes to intelligence, the whole can indeed be greater than the sum of its parts as individual intelligence was less important for successful projects than collective intelligence. That collective intelligence, the researchers believe, stems from how well the group works together. It was also noted that in groups that were dominated by one individual, the group was less collectively intelligent than in groups where the conversations were more evenly distributed. In terms of diversity, the study also found that the group performance improved when the proportion of women increased potentially based on their perceived increased predictive powers.

According to the latest edition of the National Science Foundation's biennial report, "Women, Minorities, and Persons with Disabilities in Science and Engineering.", while the U.S. population is becoming more diverse, this is not reflected in STEM profession participation. Among its findings:

- 51% of the scientists and engineers working in the U.S. are white males, even though they only represent 31.3% of the U.S. population
- Although women represent 50.9% of the total U.S. population, they only account for 28% of the science and engineering workforce
- The number of underrepresented minorities studying engineering and the physical sciences has stayed relatively flat since the year 2000
- The percentage of women working in computer science and engineering is not just low, it is declining
- Unemployment rates are significantly higher for minority scientists and engineers
- More black doctorate recipients go into agriculture and physical sciences than engineering or computer sciences

Companies that diversify their workforces in the global economy will have a distinct competitive advantage over those that don't. How are you equipped to manage the complexity and challenges of a rapidly evolving global business environment?

Reaching out to the Crowd

American journalist Henry Mencken once stated that "no one in this world, so far as I known, has ever lost money by underestimating the intelligence of the great masses of the plain people". Technology-enabled 21st collaboration can reach out to those masses of people to draw our diverse and global community closer together. These masses or crowds of people can do amazing things. Through the aggregation of thousands of contributions made by virtual crowds have been shown to innovate through their collective wisdom.

Consider the development of Linux - the free and open source Unix-like operating system that was traced to Linus Torvalds. Although Torvalds was the chief architect of the Linux, he couldn't have succeeded without the power of the crowd. It's been estimated that he only wrote approximately 2% of the operating system's code.

In 2006, the term "Crowd sourcing" was coined by Jeff Howe of Wired magazine to describe how the Internet has enabled large, distributed teams of amateurs to do work that was previously the domain of isolated experts or corporations.

The applicability of Crowd sourcing is virtually endless and has been applied to the following business areas:

- Advertising and Marketing
- New Product Development
- Software Development
- Generating Content
- Fundraising
- Skilled Labor
- Research

A representative set of the many dozens of successful Crowd sourcing initiatives:

- The Frito Lay's "Do Us A Flavor" contest asked customers to come up with a new potato-chip flavor.
- The not-for-profit Wikipedia Foundation offers a free, web-based, collaborative encyclopedia. This has become the most popular reference site on the Internet as it contains

over 10 million articles in over 200 languages that were written collaboratively by the global community.

- Amazon's Mechanical Turk is termed 'a marketplace for work' that offers businesses and developers access to an on-demand scalable workforce. These Internet-based technology tasks are organized and performed by a 'crowd' with people who wish to be part of the 'crowd' performing those tasks. Tasks or projects are organized into HITs (Human Intelligence Tasks) and performed by workers who choose them from a list.

- Source Forge is a web-based source code repository that offers a centralized location for software developers to control and manage free and open source software development activities.

- Luxury automaker BMW through their Customer Innovation Lab 1045 lets participants share their ideas with regard to innovative telematics and online services as well as driver assistance systems of the future. In this crowd sourced environment, participants made suggestions in a structured multimedia environment, which enabled them to view, evaluate and build upon proposals made by other participants. Through such previous Customer Innovation Labs, captured ideas were realized by BMW and introduced into new products.

Foldit is a unique computer game that actually enables anyone to contribute to scientific research into the way proteins are formed. This in turn can help in research to find cures for serious illnesses such as Alzheimer's and AIDS. In Foldit, players around the world compete to design proteins. In the next step, real scientists actually test the proteins designed by the game's players to see if they make viable candidate compounds for new drugs.

NASA has announced its Asteroid Grand Challenge, which according to NASA Deputy Administrator Lori Garver is "focused on detecting and characterizing asteroids and learning how to deal with potential threats. We will also harness public engagement, open innovation and citizen science to help solve this global problem." (NASA news releases, 2013)

An open question to any leader is how crowd sourcing impacts your strategy and business plans. There are numerous possibilities for crowd sourcing your business. Crowd sourcing has both benefits and risks to extend your enterprise that must be weighted.

Benefits
- R&D and problem-solving at minimal or no cost
- Draw more attention and exposure to your organization
- Its utilization as an on-demand virtual workforce that will easily allow the purchase cheap labor on a global scale
- Reduced unit labor costs
- Companies gain consumer insights
- Harness the global talent pool
- Discover new and competent talent and energy outside of the organization
- Full rights are gained to the materials
- Motivate your internal workforce

Risks
- Not at projects are appropriate for crowd sourcing
- The impact of 'outsourcing' innovation outside of the organization with its impact on the internal workforce.
- The costs required to sort through each submission
- The additional hidden costs required to reach satisfactory results
- No confidentiality – showing your competitors what your organization is up to and providing them your ideas.
- Too few participants and potentially coming up empty
- Trust in the results
- Poor quality entries

- Not reaching the proper talent

Another form of reaching out to the crowd is through Crowd funding. Crowd funding is "the practice of funding a project or venture by raising many small amounts of money from a large number of people, typically via the Internet. Any individual or group can propose an innovative, entrepreneurial ideas and ventures that require funding allowing other interested parties to contribute funds in its support. This Internet-based funding portal sometimes goes by different names such as crowd capital, crowd raising, or crowd financing and other similar terms. Crowd funding is recognized as a legalized entity per the Crowd fund Act of 2012 (part of the JOBS Act). Crowd funding is not only useful funding opportunity for small businesses or startups as it also provides a great outlet for more established companies who are looking for additional capital to expand their product range.

Social media successfully dovetails with Crowd sourcing to allow organizations to reach a wider audience faster, cheaper and more efficiently than ever before. Both the wisdom and capital of clouds can change your business. Can you see where this may be applicable?

Diverse Teams Improve Innovation

Why is it that our star performers do not necessarily create star teams? Is it even possible to improve the collective intelligence of a team and make them more innovative? That's the question that a team of academics set for themselves.

Being a team themselves, of course they believed in collective intelligence but the harder question was: can it be measured? Is there a group equivalent of IQ? Can the collective intelligence of the group as a whole go above and beyond the abilities of the individual group members? And, if it can, what factors contribute to making a team smarter?

In two studies with 699 people, teams were set tasks that involved solving visual puzzles, brainstorming, making collective moral judgments, and negotiating over limited resources. The same tasks were given to individuals and then to teams. The collective intelligence of the group (which they called "c") far out-performed the average intelligence of individual participants. That makes sense; it's why we do team work in the first place. But what the researchers most wanted to know was: what predicted "c"? What was it that might give any particular group greater collective intelligence?

Their findings are intriguing, provocative and profound. Collective intelligence is not strongly correlated with the average or the maximum individual intelligence of group members. Packing your teams with one, or a few, super smart people may not help you. Furthermore, group cohesion, motivation and satisfaction also did not determine group performance. What did make a difference were:

- Social sensitivity of group members: Teams in which members understood each other's mood did better than teams that lacked that sensitivity.

- Equality in distribution of conversational turn taking: The groups where a few people dominated the conversation were less collectively intelligent than those where participants more equally shared the floor.

- The proportion of women in the group: The researchers thought that this finding might be connected to the other two, since women tended to do better on sensitivity tests and be good at taking turns.

These findings are important to everyone who isn't a hermit. They have powerful implication for the skills we seek when hiring and for the tools we use for collaboration. It means that the colleague who does all the talking isn't just annoying - he may, quite literally, be lowering the tone of the conversation. More importantly, the researchers argue it may be easier to raise the collective intelligence -"c"- of a group than the IQ of an individual because how smart a group is depends on its membership.

But most important of all, it reinforces everything everyone has ever said about the case for greater gender diversity at all levels of an organization: namely, diversity makes companies smarter. And this work wasn't published in a magazine for managers, HR professionals or women. It appeared in SCIENCE. In other words, it isn't wishful thinking. It is peer reviewed, analyzed and tested as stringently as possible. It's based on real experiments and hard data. There isn't a manager in the world that doesn't need to read it.

Are you part of a diverse team, and how does it impact your ability to innovate?

Speed and Impact of Business Change

Constant change is the new dynamic for business. Never in our history have leaders experienced the scale and complexity of change that they now face. Consider the competition that business face in the global economy. New unforeseen factors, such as terrorism or pandemic outbreaks can have major impacts. Disruptive innovations and rapid technological advancements are influencing all aspects of the business world, from marketing and networking to research and development. And all of these are being played out at the same time. Your success as a leader is measured by the speed of producing results and bringing new realities into existence.

An IBM ad in 2011 noted that of the top 25 industrial corporations in the America of 1900, only two survived to the 1960s. Of the top 25 on the Fortune 500 list today, only several remain. These sobering statistics show just how tough it is to keep a business on course. Every company must recognize the need to evolve in order to adopt new technologies, products and business strategies as the market changes to ensure continued growth. This has become a game of survival where successful leaders need to demonstrate the ability to create new opportunities rather than wait for them to appear.

In this fast paced environment, business leaders are held more accountable for the immediate impact of their actions. BusinessDictionary.com defines accountability as "the obligation of an individual or organization to account for its activities, accept responsibility for them, and to disclose the results in a transparent manner". (Definitions / Accountability)

In her book *Fearless Leadership*, Loretta Malandro, states that, for a business to evolve and change, there must be a strong culture of 100 percent accountability where everyone must share and accept that commitment, regardless of their position within the organization. She defines this as "being personally accountable for business results and your impact on people, even when others accept zero accountability." Accountability is about standing tall and acting decisively, even in the face of adversity and your willingness to accept the consequences – either good or bad. This form of personal leadership can reduce the obstacles in dealing with your team. (Malandro, 2009)

Another view of speed is that is a cultural rather than technical issue. It's convincing everyone in the organization that his or her survival depends on moving as fast as possible. Companies don't survive unless they're agile and innovative. As aptly stated by Norm Augustine: "Every morning in Africa a gazelle wakes up". It knows it must outrun the fastest lion or it will be killed. Every morning in Africa a lion wakes up. It knows it must outrun the gazelle or it will starve. It doesn't matter whether you're a lion or a gazelle---When the sun comes up, you'd better be running"

In his book, The Agenda, business process guru, Dr. Michael Hammer focuses on showing how companies can prosper in today's turbulent business climate. "Globalization led to more companies pursuing the same customers. At the same time, customers have become more sophisticated and informed buyers. Information technology enabled them to find and analyze competing products and to make intelligent choices. Customers discovered they had options and the power to exploit them. Customers now aggressively seek alternatives, compare offers, and hold out for the best option." (Hammer, 2003)

Communication Technology Impact on Business

Communications technologies such as the Internet, and Wi-Fi in concert with handheld portable electronic devices (i.e., cell phones and tablets) are potent communication tools, offers global reach, unprecedented speed and business change. They have become a major game changer, just as the telegraph, the telephone eventually did to facilitate communications practices in years past.

As technology is evolving so rapidly, organizations need to focus beyond today's or yesterday's technology and look toward the future.

The rapidity in which we are able to communicate spurred the catchphrase "Internet time" that was developed during the 1990's Internet boom. People who used the Internet had come to believe that "everything moved faster on the 'net'", because the Internet made the dissemination of information far more efficient and less expensive. Time and distance continue to become less and less relevant thanks in significant part due to the explosive growth of technology and the Internet.

In Internet Time, news, information, business data, policies and all of their respective consequences travel the world at the speed of light.

All businesses depend on effective and timely communication. In the past, it would take costly measures to overcome the distance barrier. Email has had a major impact on business and society by creating almost instant communications by offering greater convenience than the old methods of "snail mail", telephone calls or face-to-face meetings.

Some basic email usage facts (email usage) are:

- 144.8 Billion emails are sent worldwide per day, 89 Billion in business and 55.8B in personal.
- 3.3 Billion registered email accounts as of 2012 and 75% consumer accounts and 25% business accounts.
- 90 Million of Americans access emails through a mobile device and 82% access from Smartphone and send email on their phones.
- 65% of all emails sent are spam, but filters catch most of it.
- 11.2 Hours average time spent reading and answering emails per week with 28% of a 40-hour work (email usage)

Emails are just one form of communication that is dominating our society and became the precursor for a new wave of Internet-based interaction. Social media refers to the means of interactions among people in which they create, share, discuss, and exchange information in virtual communities with user-generated content. This introduces substantial and pervasive changes to communication businesses, communities and individuals.

Social Media Impact on Business

Businesses are now beginning to recognize the benefit of social media as a communication platform that facilitates two-way communication between an organization and its stakeholders or end user clients. Conventional product and marketing models would assemble focus groups and perform surveys to solicit consumer feedback. This approach can be expensive, time-consuming, and difficult to measure in real time. Today, two-thirds of large businesses surveyed now use advanced Web 2.0 tools such as social networks or blogs, with use of internal social networks up 50% since 2008, according to a survey by McKinsey & Co. Nearly 90%

said they have reaped at least one measurable business benefit, though most say the improvements have been modest. (The Rise of the Networked Enterprised - Web 2.0 finds its Payday, 2010)

Forrester Research says the sales of software to run corporate social networks will grow 61% a year and be a $6.4 billion business by 2016. (Social Media is reinvesnting how business is done, 2012)

According to Nielsen, Internet users continue to spend more time with social media sites than any other type of site. At the same time, the total time spent on social media in the U.S. across PC and mobile devices increased by 37 percent to 121 billion minutes in July 2012 compared to 88 billion minutes in July 2011. (Social Media Report 2012, 2012)

This supports company processes and objectives including Customer Relationship Management (CRM), product marketing, market research, customer base expansion retention, CX metrics, connecting with employees, supplier coordination, and recruiting. Heavy use of social tools has a statistically significant correlation to profitability, said Michael Chui, senior fellow at the McKinsey Global Institute.

Another important factor is the dissemination of news and information. In pre-Internet times, there was the day-by-day pace of the news cycle of printed daily newspapers. As technology progressed, radio and then television became the primary communication media. Today, news sources on the World Wide Web (including Blogs) and the advent of 24-hour cable and satellite television news channels have considerably shortened this process.

Even corporate leadership can be impacted by Social Media. By collaborating on Glassdoor, the employees of thousands of companies can share salary information and express their opinions about the organization and its leadership through anonymous postings. Services such as StockTwits use social media data to gauge how passionate investors feel about a company.

The contrast between social media and your more traditional news source media differs in many aspects such as quality, usability, frequency, immediacy and permanence. The normal human reaction to such a rapid pace of change is to be overwhelmed, stressed out, anxious and fearful.

Cloud Computing Impact on Business

A storm is brewing and the business forecast is Cloudy. Cloud computing is the latest major evolution in computing. Cloud computing isn't a new set of technologies or architectures, it's a new 21st century business model with on-demand business innovation. According to GE CTO, Gregory Simpson, "The Cloud is nothing more than the platform upon which to build better businesses". This new IT delivery model lets the business leader better focus on core business matters rather than worry about which new technology should be purchased. Simply defined, it is a paradigm where computing resources are available when needed, and you pay for their use in much the same way as for household utilities. Cloud computing shifts focus from IT-based products, to business oriented services.

Clouds offer a full range of computing services that are generally offered by a Cloud Service Provider (CSP). Here are examples of cloud computing impact on business:

- Ultimate Flexibility – Massive scalability and elasticity with organizations paying only for what they use; IT costs are directly proportional to usage requirements, growing and shrinking as needs change.
- Ease of Procurement and Installation - The conventional IT model for requesting IT resources (e.g., servers) was to wait for weeks or months for the request to wind its way through the procurement, cycle, delivery, installation and the final establishment of the required IT environment. With the cloud computing paradigm, developers can now unilaterally provision compute and network storage in real-time

without having to go to the operations team. Developers can now bypass Operations by setting up their own cloud-based development, test and production environments. This results in businesses not losing unnecessary time and speeding up ultimate time to product or service delivery.

- Reduced Operational Expenses – Due to a high degree of automation, businesses do not need to set up a team to handle system updates, maintenance, and back-ups. IT departments will discover that cloud deployments allow for a renewed focus on core competencies.

- On-Demand Business Services - A growing number of organizations are investing in Software-as-a-Service (SaaS). This deployment model is changing the way cloud-based services are consumed by the lines of business. A prime example of this is Microsoft Office. In the past, Office would be installed and maintained on every PC within an organization. Today, with Office 365, an organization has access to the latest software version through the cloud.

- Self-Service – Businesses will be able to have less direct involvement with the IT department in adopting cloud solutions.

- Innovation Initiatives – Startup expenses for innovation initiatives can be reduced through the use of the cloud to test out new ideas and nurture them.

- Cloud computing helps businesses become mobile – Business wants to make employees productive, especially in an increasingly real time world. A new term Mobile Cloud Computing has been devised for the synergistic combination of cloud computing and mobile applications. In mobile cloud computing, data processing and storage occurs outside the mobile device in the cloud and results are displayed on the mobile device. Business users are able to share resources and applications without a high level of capital expenditure on hardware and software resources.

- An On-ramp to new computing advances – new technical innovations such as non-relational databases, social networking tools, and big data frameworks are now available on-line.

Cloud computing is attractive to many business leaders due to its scalability, ease of management and low costs. Cloud migration, sometimes referred to as Business Process outsourcing (BPO), is the process of partially or completely deploying an organization's digital assets, services, IT resources or applications to the cloud. The migrated assets are accessible behind the cloud's firewall.

Cloud computing can be provided within an existing enterprise datacenter or it can be delivered as a service through a Cloud Service Provider. To facilitate organization lack of experience with cloud computing, Cloud service aggregators, or brokers, are beginning to emerge to help those organizations. This can be especially helpful in multi-cloud environments. The Service brokers sit between the cloud and the client to actually package all of the services based on the needs (service levels and governance) of the organization.

21st Century Innovation Brings Speed to Knowledge

When we think about innovation, we typically think about the result, not the process, as if the idea sprang out of the ground fully formed. Innovation is not getting something to market; it's getting the right product or service to market. This requires a commitment to the consumer, not solely to your company's internal capabilities. It is speed to knowledge of what your customers want that matters, not just speed to deployment. True innovation takes a bit of planning.

We're all familiar with famous innovators such as Steve Jobs and Howard Schultz, but the truth is we're all innovators. It's behavior more than it is a gift. Fundamentally, it's about problem solving, understanding how to ask the right questions, and seeing patterns before facts.

There are four principles necessary to hold to in order to preserve what's essential about a brand without closing minds to the innovative opportunities a new product presents.

1. Define what you're bringing to market, starting with the brand purpose. How do you interpret your brand based on the role it already plays in people's lives? How do you create a new proposition that extends and reinterprets your brand? The first step is asking the right questions. Identify which trends are indicative of changing consumer needs, How can you affect both consumer behavior and the bottom line? Why are you going to be relevant in consumers' daily lives?

2. Once you've identified the idea, how do you build consensus, create believers, and drive momentum? Place these new ideas in the parameters of your brand from the start. While this shouldn't be restricting, you need to be sure your innovative ideas will not erode your brand.

3. The key battle to differentiating is balancing your intuition with certainty. It's not just about what makes you competitively distinct. It's what you stand for in people's lives.

4. Great brands think about the entire engagement of the innovation and improve every aspect, not solely the product. Remember that packaging is not an afterthought, and it's not just an execution: It's the most tangible touch point the consumer has with your brand.

As innovators we need to trust in our gut but then ask the right questions. We need to identify the opportunities in front of us and recognize the right way to tap the brand equities we have in hand.

Sometimes innovation is about reinterpreting—not reinventing the way we talk to consumers.

As innovators, how do you bring speed to knowledge?

Rapid technology change impacting innovation

It's safe to say that at no point in history has technology changed so rapidly and created so many opportunities and risks. What's particularly unsettling about today's post-PC environment is that the rules and wisdom of the past often don't apply.

Nowhere is this more apparent than in managing the various sales and marketing channels that now exist. Once upon a time, enterprises communicated with customers in person, using the phone and via snail mail. Marketers placed ads in print, TV and radio, and used direct mail to interact with consumers.

Today, mobile technology is changing everything. It's not so much that social media; geolocation information, big data and other tools exist and require their own set of applications and strategies. It's that they create a three-dimensional chess game that's infinitely more complex and unpredictable. Brands and reputations soar or stumble in a matter of minutes in a world where consumers suddenly wield as much power as corporations.

That much you probably know. But what many business and IT leaders don't fully grasp is that channel integration must be approached from the customer's perspective rather than that of the enterprise. In this brave new world, the technology and devices used to access a company or an account are irrelevant for consumers. It's simply a matter of having a ubiquitous view of purchases, loyalty points, coupons and social media ties. Essentially, consumers want their favorite brands to follow them around everywhere, all the time.

In a business and IT world mired in legacy systems and cost controls, making the technology invisible aren't easily done. Success requires more than building out robust channels or tossing out mobile apps. It requires more than achieving goals for metrics. High click rates and hugely successful viral campaigns don't necessarily lead to bottom-line results.

Today, the most innovative leaders crumple silos. They put big data to use in new and inventive ways. They create micro-incubators for innovation and find people who can serve as "intrapreneurs". They use big data, crowd sourcing and bottoms-up methods to identify new products and services that customers didn't know they wanted—and the business never thought of providing. They create marketing and sales channels that work so well that they're there, but they're not apparent to the consumer.

Agile and Flexible Organization Structures

Due to the speed and impact of business change, agility is even more necessary than at any point in business history. Agility is the catalyst for business results. The need for transformation from today's inflexible business environment to an agile enterprise that can change direction rapidly has never been greater. Yet in many cases, the structures, processes and systems that are in place today are inflexible: they are incapable of rapid change.

Agility can be defined as the power of moving quickly, easily and nimbly. Within Information Technology, agility is reflected in the Agile Programming paradigm which promotes processes that accommodate changing business requirements, stakeholder collaboration, high-performing software development teams, and software delivery in short iterations. Leadership agility is now also becoming a word increasingly heard in business domain based on market forces such as globalization, information technology, and deregulation. From a business perspective, agility is the ability of a business to adapt rapidly in response to a dynamic business environment by providing goods and services that meet ever-changing customer demands.

We live in an incredible era of possibility where change is everywhere and constant for all leaders. "It's not the strongest nor most intelligent of the species that survive; it is the one most adaptable to change." ~ Charles Darwin. The use of an organizations most crucial asset – its employee knowledge, can play a role in problem solving.

According to a recent study by the Leadership Workshop Profile Report, "Flexibility, agility, and innovation are qualities most leaders and organizations want to acquire or amplify." This report cites a 2010 IBM CEO study, which showed two primary themes emerging based on interviews of over 1,500 CEO's worldwide. The first theme was managing complexity and the second was developing the creative capacity in the organization to innovate in response to the shifting marketplace demands. (Report, 2010)

The alignment between business objectives of an organization and the Information Technology (IT) requirements of an enterprise is crucial to the overall success of an enterprise. An organization must be flexible to new technologies that are creating a new wave of innovation. These technological innovations need to drive your business outcomes to help influence new strategies and engagements. An organization often doesn't change until its leaders do.

In his book, "Straight from the Gut, Change before you have to" Jack Welch says in his 20 years at the helm, he took GE with a market capitalization of about $12 billion to a market value of about $500 billion. He has utilized a very human process to drive change through GE's vast organization. Welch was an advocate of flat organizational structures, operating without command and control hierarchies, to be more responsive and agile to the new complex, fast-paced, global environment.

Leadership is a necessary workplace variable as it builds structure within an organization. Every business structure, bureaucracy and control mechanisms will differ just as each business has unique needs. What must be considered first is the building of a structure and who will be involved in the structure.

An organizational structure can be rigid, flexible or something in between. Rigid organizations employ the functional structure, which typically features many management layers. This form of structure can hamper agility. The moral is to be fast and decisive in making business decisions without being encumbered by the bureaucracy of the organization. Most people want 'elbow room', whereby they are provided a degree of responsibility as well as 'headroom', where they can make decisions on their own, without having to go through layers of bureaucracy.

An agile enterprise changes these relationships by breaking down departmental silos into sharable service units. The participation and relationships of people continue to be important in the agile enterprise, but the focus has shifted from performing production tasks to more flexibly address business challenges and opportunities. According to Norman Augustine, "If sufficient numbers of management layers are superimposed on top of each other, it can be assured that disaster is not left to chance". To further accentuate the need for agility in business, the founder of Electronic Data Systems and later Perot Systems, H Ross Perot, once noted, "If you see a snake, just kill it. Don't appoint a committee on snakes."

Companies that never saw it coming

There is a difference between having a recognizable icon brand name and having a solid and agile business to back it up. There are numerous companies that have foundered, shrunk, grown obsolete, or been acquired by rivals that grew stronger. A reason that why companies cannot afford to fall behind in maintaining their flexibility is demonstrated in the following list

Pan Am, whose slogan was the "World's Most Experienced Airline," was once the largest international air carrier in the United States. As an industry innovator, it was the first airline to implement a computerized reservation systems, realize the importance of well-trained crews, worldwide flights, and the of use jet planes. Numerous management missteps and external events lead to their ultimate demise.

Research in Motion (RIM) is known for its development of the Blackberry Smartphone. While once the leader in the entire corporate market, they failed to adapt their technology for consumer use along with having dated technology. This once innovative company lost its edge to the Apple iPhone and other Smartphone offerings.

Legendary camera and filmmaker, Kodak continues to face a fuzzy future. Unfortunately, the company was not agile or visionary enough to jump on the digital bandwagon, despite inventing the first solid-state image sensors that converted light into digital pictures. This undermined the fundamental business model of Kodak, which meant cannibalizing its then very profitable film business. When Kodak did enter the market, its rivals kept innovating over the years with features like face detection and in-camera red-eye fixes. While Kodak offered competent products, they were was always following feature trends, never leading them and were not as appealing to the consumer.

The once powerful Internet company that helped usher in the age of the Internet and "You've Got Mail", America Online (AOL) still exists but as a shadow of its former self.

Successful companies tend to fall into three traps that make the glory days fleeting, says Vijay Govindarajan, professor at Dartmouth's Tuck School of Business and co-author of The Other Side of Innovation, These are the physical trap (e.g., continued investments in legacy systems and processes which hamper more relevant investments); the psychological trap (e.g., a preoccupation on their current successful product and ignoring new areas that may displace it); and the strategic trap (e.g., failing to anticipate the future). (Vijay Govindarajan, 2010)

If a company keeps offering the same product, a rival can easily leap forward with one that is incrementally better. But yet another competitor can blow them both out of the water when they invent something innovative. Companies must consider how to find and retain visionary leaders and how to foster innovation and creativity in their employees in order to remain competitive. These basic lessons apply to small as well as large companies.

You'll find that the list of companies that have faltered over the past 50 years is extensive. How many former household name companies can you remember?

The Knowledge Worker

The industrial age with its automation of factories and farms has freed large parts of the workforce from having to perform physical labor. The advent of the computer and information age has created a demand for those people that had new skills. These events have resulted in the emergence of a new type of worker referred to as the Knowledge worker as coined by Peter Drucker in 1955. Drucker intended the term to describe a successor class to factory workers, but now we can define knowledge workers as participants in the knowledge economy. This successor class of knowledge workers has become the knowledge organization, which requires new leadership approaches.

"The great challenge to management today is to make productive the tremendous new resource, the knowledge worker. This, rather than the productivity of the manual worker, is the key to economic growth and economic performance in today's society." (Drucker, 1993)

A knowledge worker's main asset is the knowledge and skills that they bring to an organization. Typical examples may include engineers, scientists, software programmers, healthcare practitioners, and analysts because they "think for a living". (Davenport, 2005)

As businesses increase their dependence on information technology, the number of knowledge workers required in an organization has increased dramatically. The knowledge worker is a growing sector in the workforce. The comprehensive nature of a knowledge work in today's workplace requires virtually all workers to obtain some higher degree of training or education.

An organization's ability to retain knowledge workers is a critical component in determining its present and future success. If the knowledge can be retained, a knowledge worker's contributions will serve to expand the knowledge assets of an organization. Additionally, if an organization's culture and practices do not adequately reward competitive behavior, key knowledge workers may simply elect not to share their experiences. Workplace policies that improve employee retention can help companies reduce their turnover costs. And while most companies recognize, the high costs of turnover, they don't necessarily believe that top leadership or management make a difference. Upon asking employees what it would take to improve employee retention, leader-related behaviors are typically cited. A common theme with Human Resources personnel is that employees leave their bosses, not their jobs. (Schyns, 2010). Today's workers want more involvement in decision-making, greater appreciation, improved communication, flexible work conditions, and greater autonomy. However, the failure to retain of key talent who leave without their knowledge being acquired can be a major loss that is growing in significance. Further leadership challenges in dealing with increasing job mobility coupled with baby boomer retirements.

A game changer today is the confluence of business, technology, innovation, and leadership in the way that we work. Many knowledge workers now have more options on how and when they work, and can access to more tools to meet their work needs than ever before. Gone are the days of a 9-to-5 job, thanks to the ubiquitous Internet, laptops, tablets, Smartphone's and Wi-Fi. As long as you have Internet connectivity, a knowledge worker can telecommute, communicate with co-workers, hold video teleconferences, and perform work tasks remotely. Furthermore, teams are increasingly becoming geographically dispersed and multi-cultural. Aside from the enterprise IT issues, this places additional challenges on leadership to manage their virtual and mobile teams in keeping them focused and dedicated while keeping organizational data secure. Today's new knowledge worker can be characterized as requiring the skills shown in Figure 3.

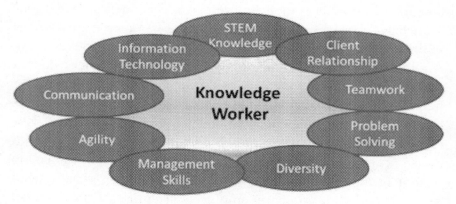

The Knowledge Worker Skill Set

Every employee within an organization should be considered a knowledge worker and should not be stifled by the management structure. Any employee might have input that can help develop better products or services and improve business performance and execution. According to Malcolm Gladwell, "Insight is not a light bulb that goes off inside of our heads. It is a flickering candle that can easily be snuffed out." (Gladwell, 2007)

The real value of a knowledge worker goes beyond their expected output. It's passing along the ideas and inspiration that drove those outcomes. Those ideas can be innovative and transformative to the business.

Knowledge workers are performing well below their potential because companies still don't know how to manage them, according to Thomas Davenport, professor of information technology and management at Babson College. "Knowledge workers are going to be the primary force determining which economies are successful and which aren't. They are the key source of growth in most organizations. New products and services, new approaches to marketing, new business models—all these come from knowledge workers. So if you want your economy to grow, your knowledge workers had better be doing a good job." (Alter, 2005)

A true leader needs to take steps to ensure that their knowledge workers can be utilized optimally and to maintain high levels of performance with the following steps:

- Ensure that a culture of knowledge sharing is part of the organization's mission statement.
- Regardless of their tasking, don't leave your people alone. Some organizations believe in recruiting and hiring smart people and then ultimately leaving them in a vacuum and in a perceived rut. In the industrial age, the primary value of a worker was "to do" with everyone conforming to the same standard and potentially mindless or "by rote" way of doing something. Today, in the postindustrial age, a knowledge worker's greatest value is from their mental ability "to think". As this new form of worker's value is intellectual, conforming to rigid work standards and structures, doesn't work well. Just as with manual labor, knowledge work can also become mundane and unfulfilling. Therefore, all too frequently, there are workers that are frustrated, unfulfilled and not passionate about their work. All workers require some form of continuing nurturing from and collaboration with their leadership chain.

- Provide continuous learning and performance improvement opportunities. Ensure that the right level of training is in place through a variety of options from Just In Time learning through After Hours on-line training courses, that workers can take at their own pace and own self-designated time. Also offer the ability for knowledge workers to learn as an integral part of their normal job workflow.

- Provide access to the same data and information to all employees. This form of information equality encourages sharing and sparks collaboration across the organization. The culture of "openness" of the organization is seen as a crucial factor.

- Break down existing barriers within the organization.

- The physical barriers of globally dispersed organizations due to geographic distance and time zones can't be changed.

- Leveraging information technology to enable spontaneous collaboration through the utilization of social media tools can break down the technical barriers. The role of tools is central in accessing and sharing information in a 21st century organization and make sure that your knowledge workers have the appropriate technology available to them. The advent of the mobile workforce accentuates the need for these tools. By supplementing these tools with video conferencing and virtual collaboration, organizations can bridge physical distances and build relationships.

- The cultural, working norms, or social barriers, such as rigid hierarchy, don't spur a knowledge worker to effectively engage. To alleviate these barriers, solutions such as incorporating "knowledge sharing" as a metric within performance reviews, is a simple option. Other recommendations would be to enlighten workers about the workings of the organizational structure and the importance of collaborative problem solving.

- The contextual barrier represents a misunderstanding of the roles and capabilities of people within different aspects of the organization. This disparity can be based on different vocabularies and knowledge. The use of business forums or short videos that highlight different aspects of the organization and how they work can benefit.

- The structural barrier is based on traditional organizations that are based on a tiered hierarchy with uni-directional flow of operational commands emanating from the top down. This also represents a knowledge hierarchy that inhibits the flow of operational knowledge and strategies to the knowledge workers. Knowledge workers need to be provided "the big picture" view. Through the deeper insight provided by a leader, there is an increase in "connectedness" an buy-in to the work at hand.

- The bureaucracy barrier is dealing with the rigid formalized structures that are a part of many organizations. The formalities of the organizational structure must be ignored for information to be provided to the correct individuals.

- Note multiculturalism and diversity in your dealings. In this brave new world, don't use the same template in dealing with every knowledge worker. Treating everyone the same way may miss opportunities in garnering innovation or enhanced productivity from them.

- Utilize the appropriate workflow and decision-making approach to facilitate overall knowledge worker effectiveness. Dependent on the tasking and personnel location, workers and tasks may be geographically dispersed and require different leadership and coordination techniques.

- Provide a degree of control to the knowledge worker. Allowing knowledge workers to override automated or semi-automated decisions can provide a degree of autonomy and self-worth to the knowledge worker. Such measures can lead to better and more rapid decisions without running them "up the flagpole".

- Insure that all levels in the organization are involved and act in a timely fashion. Information should flow freely and rapidly through the organization. Everyone should have open access to everyone else within the organization.

- Recognize and reward knowledge worker input. It's generally been recognized that monetary reward is not the most important.

- Measure knowledge worker productivity. While knowledge work is difficult to measure, it must be identified and captured through a set of some key performance indicators.

According the Mark McDonald of the Gartner Group business leaders need to look at the evolution of the knowledge worker to a new type of worker – the judgment worker. "A judgment worker is someone who creates value through making decisions based on their experience, contextual awareness and subject matter expertise." According to Mark, a judgment worker makes unstructured decisions based on continually evolving information as opposed to knowledge workers who deal in a more structured framework and processes. (McDonald, 2011)

Finding Key Talent

True innovation and competitive advantage stems from a company's workforce. Hiring good and talented people can help make or break your business. Competition for top-level talent is always fierce. Talent is defined as the "natural ability to excel at a duty or action". (definition/talent)

However, the word 'talent' is sometimes loosely used and difficult to define when referring to a workforce. Given different perspectives within and across organizations, educational levels and skills, workforce and cultural diversity, different attributes are emphasized when defining key talent.

Most people use talent and skill interchangeably but they are not the same. Skill is the ability to do something well that is usually gained and improved upon through training or experience over a period of time. People can be skilled but not particularly talented.

Everybody has an opportunity to learn and earn a particular skill whereas a talent is the inherent or inborn ability to do something without prior experience or training. An individual can be driven to success in life through use of both skill and talent. However, skill is not a substitute for talent.

Today, the most differentiating and desirable attributes in a talent search include innovation, thought leadership, and the ability to lead teams. Larry Bossidy, CEO of AlliedSignal noted, "At the end of the day, we bet on people, not strategies."

Through the ubiquitous Internet and strong connected on social media, organization can increasingly leverage technology, via video interviews, online assessments and social referral recruiting tools, to source and assess key talent. . Social media can significantly expand the applicant pool and shed valuable light on job candidates. Organizations also need to utilize other approaches to fill their talent pipeline. Some organizations send representatives to conferences and community events for speaking engagements or to act as 'company ambassadors'. Supporting groups and events that specifically cater to the search for diverse potential job candidates should not be ignored. Additionally, relationships with local colleges and university can be beneficial for tapping into talent.

In considering the challenges involved in finding the right talent, think of what Capital One CEO Richard Fairback, once said: "At most companies, people spend two percent of their time recruiting and 75 percent managing their recruiting mistakes."

It's really about finding the right people for your organization. According to Gallup Chairman and CEO Jim Clifton, four types of people drive innovation: inventors, entrepreneurs, extreme individual achievers in their fields (such as the arts, entertainment, or sports), and super mentors. "The theory is that where these people settle is where new economic empires will be built," Clifton said. "And they go where there is other talent like them."

Gallup studies have also noted that there are three types of employees within an organization: Engaged (e.g., work with passion and drive innovation); Not Engaged (e.g., put in time at work but are effectively "checked-out"); and those that are Actively Disengaged (e.g. displeased and actively undermine business activity). A true leader that can create and nurture an environment where employees are engaged will ultimately yield a higher crop of creativity and innovation.

According to a 2012 IBM CEO Study, CEOs consistently highlight four personal characteristics most critical for employees' future success are being collaborative, having strong communication skills, exhibit creativity, and be flexible. (Leading Through Connections CEO Case Study, 2012) The flexibility characteristic reflects the need for finding employees with the ability to constantly reinvent themselves. Businesses are constantly evolving and new technologies are making an impact, new skills and processes are required to cope. Associated with flexibility is the ability for employees to be comfortable with change.

As numerous studies throughout the years have shown, CEOs have difficulties finding people with the appropriate skill levels. This has resulted in a war for talent, which refers to an increasingly competitive landscape for not only recruiting talented employees but retaining them as well. In our highly competitive global economy, ideas are developed quickly and cheaply, and people are more willing to look for other job opportunities more often. For the most part, gone are the days of working for one company for your entire career. This leads us to what is required to manage and develop our existing talent.

Talent Management and Development

Organizations are now paying more attention on retaining talented employees and keeping them actively engaged in their work. An organization is only as strong as the people that it employees. Talented employees should feel that their employers consider them a prize worth fighting for. Talent Management is the science of using human resources to improve business value and make it possible for organizations to reach their goals. This incorporates everything that ranges from recruitment, retain, development, rewarding as well as strategic workforce planning. Unfortunately, too many organizations dismiss talent management as a short-term, tactical problem rather than being coupled to their long-term business strategy.

Companies need to make a concerted effort to proactively identify and satisfy the needs of their most critical talent. According to a survey by HR services provider Northgate Arinso (NGA), a majority of business leaders polled said they believe that identifying the right talent is critical to success, but more than half of respondents said there is a shortage of talent in their industry. "There is a real worry that there is a lack of readily available talent and that, potentially, this will impact on a business's ability to deliver its strategic vision," said NGA Vice President of Strategic Marketing Michael Custers in a statement about the results. (HR Disciplines, 2013)

Many organizations are still dealing with outmoded talent management models that did not deal with the new age of workforce diversity, multiculturalism, globalization, and rapid business change. This has resulted in a talent expectations gap which is the disparity between what companies expect from their workforce and the skills that are available in the marketplace.

Several key aspects of talent management include:

> **Key talent retention** - Make sure that their most valuable employees are engaged and satisfied with their environment (work/life balance, compensation, benefits). The goal is to reduce turnover, which is the unplanned loss of workers who voluntarily leave and whom employers would prefer to keep. Provide reasons for employees to stay within the organization and ensure that they are aligned with the culture, values, and goals of the organization.

Loyalty, engagement, and employee retention are strongly intertwined. While loyalty itself does not guarantee engagement and employee retention, it certainly is an influencing factor. Provide growth opportunities by filling positions with promising internal candidates instead of hiring from outside the organization. Understand the global workforce and diversity aspects in talent management practices as one set of policies will not apply world-wide. Note that the military is considered by many to be a good proving ground for leaders.

Leadership Succession – The process of identifying and developing individuals with the potential to replace key leadership positions to account for people that are retiring or transitioning to other roles outside of the organization. Few events in the life of an organization are as visible, critical, or stressful as when the leader leaves and is replaced by someone new. Departures may be sudden and occur with little or no warning or may be planned to allow for mentoring and a smooth transition. Jim Skinner, former CEO of McDonald's Corp., was known to tell managers: "Give me the names of two people who could succeed you." It was just one way the CEO continued the culture of succession planning at McDonald's. In their book, Built to Last: Successful Habits for Visionary Companies, (James Collins, 1990) eighteen organizations were identified that have been industry leaders for at least fifty years. It was noted that one of the key reasons for their long-term success was because of their strong focus on succession planning and leadership development. And regardless of the succession plan, every new leader brings anxiety and potential change to the organization that needs to be addressed to insure that business rhythms and operations continue normally. There is always the question about candidate selection as to whether hire from within or hire externally for a leadership role. Succession planning should begin by hiring and developing top-level talent, but external candidates should not be ruled out. A study by Matthew Bidwell at the University of Pennsylvania's Wharton School showed that external hires are 61 percent more likely to be laid off or get fired, and 21 percent more likely than internal hires to leave a job of their own accord. The outside hires also received higher pay, but got lower marks in performance reviews during their first two years on the job. (Bidwell, 2012) One factor to be considered for leadership succession is whether the same type of leader is required. Sometimes, an individual with new skills and capabilities needs to be considered to shake things up.

Career pathing - Align the personal interests, abilities, aspirations, and talents of each employee with those of the broader organization. While there are numerous reasons for an employee to leave a company, the lack of career advancement is a key factor. Some organizations have embarked on creating the role of a Chief Talent Officer (CTO) as the person responsible for acquiring, developing and retaining key individuals. The CTO must be able to influence management to implement the necessary strategies to meet their workforce goals.

Leadership Identification - While natural leaders stand out and are easy to identify, those that have leadership potential is a more difficult process. Make every attempt to identify future leaders earlier in their careers. Realize that it takes time to nurture and develop the next generation of leadership.

Measure Progress - Provide each employee with a clear job description, performance metrics, and a growth and development plan within the organization. Measure employees progress quarterly. Use predictive workforce analytics to help identify talent gaps and to better forecast capital resource needs.

Invest in Learning and Development - Provide employees with customized learning capabilities to feed their desire to improve their skills and capabilities. Just as with previously mentioned CTO position, another new title is becoming more mainstream: Chief Learning Officer or CLO. A CLO is responsible for managing the talent or development programs within an organization.

Hiring for the Long Term - Consider long term strategic plans and growth objectives to drive recruiting strategies and hiring practices.

Talent mapping - Link the talent on hand to the talent that will be needed to support growth in order to assess shortfalls or gaps. Just as organizations maintain an inventory of supplies (paper, toner, etc.) as a part of their normal business practice, they need to maintain back-up and redundant talent to address any staffing situations that may arise.

Trends - According to a Talent study by McKinsey Global Institute, there are numerous workforce issues that need to be considered. The study notes that business leaders must develop a finer-grained view of shifting labor dynamics throughout the world. Leaders need to better tune their recruitment, off shoring, and investment strategies by considering and anticipating trends in education, aging, and incomes. (Talent Tensions Ahead: A CEO Briefing, 2012)

Chapter Two

Management and Invention vs. Leadership and Innovation

Management is doing things right;
leadership is doing the right things
—Peter F. Drucker

Invention vs. Innovation: Knowing
the difference makes a difference
—Melvin Greer

L eadership and management are two of the most frequently used terms related to the operation and success of any business or organization, regardless of its products and/or services. To succinctly summarize their roles: a manager's job is to organize, administer, and coordinate to ensure than plans stay on track while a leader's job is to establish a visionary path through guidance, inspiration, and motivation.

According to "The Wall Street Journal Essential Guide to Management" by Alan Murray, "Leadership and management must go hand in hand. They are not the same thing. But they are necessarily linked, and complementary. Any effort to separate the two is likely to cause more problems than it solves".

Deemed "the dean of leadership guru's" by Forbes magazine, Warren Bennis has persuasively argued that leaders are not born – they are made. In his book "On Becoming A Leader", he believes that one can learn from failure and that to be an effective leader one must take a big picture view and consider the end result. He has collected the following list of the differences:

- The manager administers; the leader innovates.
- The manager is a copy; the leader is an original.
- The manager maintains; the leader develops.
- The manager focuses on systems and structure; the leader focuses on people.
- The manager relies on control; the leader inspires trust.
- The manager has a short-range view; the leader has a long-range perspective.
- The manager asks how and when; the leader asks what and why.
- The manager has his or her eye always on the bottom line; the leader's eye is on the horizon.
- The manager imitates; the leader originates.
- The manager accepts the status quo; the leader challenges it.
- The manager is the classic good soldier; the leader is his or her own person.
- The manager does things right; the leader does the right thing.

(Bennis, 2009)

The late management guru and top management thinker, Peter Drucker coined the term "knowledge worker." In his book, *The Age of Discontinuity,* Drucker differentiates knowledge workers from manual workers and insists that new industries will employ mostly knowledge workers. He further predicts the coming era of information technology and notes that our advanced economies must shift to depend on knowledge work rather than industrial might. One of his most famous disciples alive today is Jack Welch. Drucker identified the emergence of the "knowledge worker," and that "one does not 'manage' people. The task is to lead people. And the goal is to make productive the specific strengths and knowledge of every individual." (Drucker, 1969)

Is leadership your focus, without wanting to take on the responsibilities of a manager; is management in your future; or are you committed to being both a leader and a manager as your professional career progresses?

Invention vs. Innovation

Invention is often viewed as a source of economic growth. It isn't. It's innovation that generates new products, new services, new businesses, and new jobs. As a country we need to be focused on innovation more than ever before. Innovation always trumps invention.

The implications of this confusion are important, steering budding entrepreneurs down the wrong path, crimping the growth of existing companies, and muddying public policy intended to support business.

Invention and innovation have been mashed together so thoroughly that it is hard to tell the difference between them—yet they could not be more different. It is time to clarify and redefine the difference between invention and innovation.

Invention is a "new scientific or technical idea, and the means of its embodiment or accomplishment. To be patentable, an invention must be novel, have utility, and be non-obvious. To be called an invention, an idea only needs to be proven as workable". (business dictionary/definition) While the transistor was probably one of the most important inventions of the 20th Century, it received little attention at the time. AT&T Bell Laboratories developed the transistor as a way to amplify long distance calls and it never realized any other significant value from the invention. In 1952, AT&T licensed the transistor for a mere $25,000 to companies that recognized its potential and ultimately reaped significant financial rewards. While AT&T did an outstanding job with the invention, but failed to develop the innovation.

Innovation is the process of translating an idea or invention into a good or service that creates value or for which customers will pay". (business dictionary/definition) This is the commercialization of the invention itself. As there may not be a consumer base ready or available to pay for the invention, not all inventions lead to innovations due to their economic viability and value.

Innovation differs from invention in that innovation refers to the use of a better and more novel idea or method, whereas invention refers more directly to the creation of the idea or method itself. To monetize an invention requires its transformation into innovation, once a target customer or market is found. Unlike invention, which often concerns a single product or process, innovation usually involves combining products and processes to allow the successful translation of "new ideas into tangible societal impact," as Krisztina Holly, executive director of the University of Southern California's Stevens Institute for Innovation, once put it. (Holly)

Consider the Apple iPod – while not inventive, it was innovative as it combined new design elements and ease of use.

The Linux Operating System (OS) can be considered an example of open innovation. The Linux OS is considered Open Source Software (OSS), which is typically created as a collaborative effort in which programmers develop and improve upon the code, and share these changes within the global community. This open source concept originated as a response to proprietary software owned by corporations. The IP policies associated with Open Source Software allows this shared technology to become available to potential users at little or no cost to use, copy, modify, sublicense, or distribute. In many cases, OSS leads innovation and is more than being just a free or low-cost alternative solution to an enterprise, having contributed much to the software landscape. For example, much of the software in use on the web today -- from the Firefox browser to the Apache Web Server to the Perl, Python, and Ruby scripting languages -- began life as open source projects.

Innovations are separated into two broad categories:

- Evolutionary or continuous innovations that are brought about by many incremental advances in technology or processes
- Revolutionary innovations, which are often disruptive and new

Innovation itself differs from improvement in that innovation refers to the notion of doing something different rather than doing the same thing better. An example of an improvement would be Dell developing a cheaper IBM compatible PC against HP. This improvement resulted in a lesser degree of risk as a more effective approach was taken with the original innovation.

Great Britain and Germany dominated scientific advancements into the 19th century. British engineers built the foundation for the Industrial Revolution, helped largely by their invention of the steam engine. German scientists developed key principles in the world of physics. This was followed from the late 19th to mid-20th centuries by the United States, when it produced such famous and revered names as Edison, Ford, Morse, among others.

According to University of Pennsylvania historian of technology Thomas P. Hughes, who explores this "golden age" of American science in his book American Genesis: A Century of Invention and Technological Enthusiasm, 1870-1970. "No other nation has displayed such inventive power and produced such brilliant innovators as the United States during the half-century that began around 1870," wrote Hughes, who noted that the number of new patents issued annually in the country more than doubled between 1866 and 1896. Hughes tried to delve into the inventor's minds to understand why independent inventors chose to solve the problems they did and how they went about solving them.

He characterized two types of inventions as "radical and system-originating" (e.g., Wright Brothers, the airplane; Lee De Forest, wireless communication; and Nikola Tesla, power transmission) or the conservative system-improving ones (e.g., Thomas Edison, the light bulb, and Elmer Sperry, the gyrocompass). (Hughes, 2004).

It's important to note that the "system-originating" innovations during this time were actual enhancements and improvements to existing technologies that were already in existence. For instance, Thomas Edison didn't invent the light bulb, but made it practical by developing the first commercially practical incandescent light. That honor goes to J. W. Starr, who filed the patent 30 years earlier. The Wright brothers were not the first men to fly but finally succeeded at Kitty Hawk in 1903. Innovation rarely happens in isolation. Rather than being lone geniuses or soloists, individuals like Edison mastered recombining others' ideas in new ways. The concept of exploiting knowledge and work performed by others in an attempt to create new solutions is sometimes referred to as recombinant innovation.

Thomas Edison continually connected with others to generate and execute ideas. There were no inventions from Menlo Park that were truly invented from nothing – each one had some basis that was pulled from another field of technology. Edison's ability to deliver "a minor invention every ten days and a big thing every six months or so" evolved because of his network and his laboratory's ability to recombine existing ideas. (Andrew Hargadon, "Brokers of Innovation: Lessons from the Past,") Albert Szent Gyorgyi, the Nobel Laureate once remarked, "Discovery is seeing what everybody else has seen, but thinking what nobody else has thought."

What was revolutionary about the Wright brothers work was neither the glider nor the engine, which both relied on existing technology, it was the idea of a glider with movable parts in the wing assembly, to vary the shape of the wing surface in response to the flight conditions In 1903, Orville and Wilbur Wright undertook the first controlled, motor driven flight, which proved the starting point for modern aviation There are many brilliant inventions that fail while other outwardly unexceptional offerings succeed.

But, often the term innovation gets confused with creativity, according to Barry Conchie, principal leadership consultant at Gallup. "Let's be clear: Innovation and creativity are not the same thing," Conchie said. "Creativity may spur innovation, but there's an element of action missing there." The difference is that innovation actually brings ideas into fruition. "You can't get innovation without a groundswell of creativity," Conchie said. "But you [must] turn creativity into something that has an impact beyond the conversation you had about the idea." (Mika, 2007)

Modern day American entrepreneur and inventor, Steve Jobs, best known as the co-founder, chairman, and CEO of Apple Inc, whose revolutionary products, which include the iPod, iPhone and iPad, are now seen as dictating the evolution of modern technology, was noted for several quotes about innovation:

- "Sometimes when you innovate, you make mistakes. It is best to admit them quickly, and get on with improving your other innovations"
- "Innovation distinguishes between a leader and a follower"
- "Creativity is just connecting things. When you ask creative people how they did something, they feel a little guilty they just saw something. It seemed obvious to them after a while. That's because they were able to connect experiences they've had and synthesize new things"
- "But innovation comes from people meeting up in the hallways or calling each other at 10:30 at night with a new idea, or because they realized something that shoots holes in how we've been thinking about a problem"

Managing any form of innovation, from a simple "good idea" to a sophisticated breakthrough game changer, is not an easy task.

"Most companies are not short on new ideas, but they are short on ways to assess, screen, prioritize, and execute those new ideas." (Ikujiro Nonaka, 1995) Ideas and innovation are continuously needed across the spectrum of a business, ranging from "high tech" engineering to marketing, customer retention, collaboration, and business practices. A single idea could make the difference between the success or failure in business. If an organization lacks a holistic approach to dealing with new ideas, innovation will suffer and resources will be wasted.

How many times have you heard:

- It's not our business
- It shouldn't be our business
- Not Invented Here (NIH)
- It's a great idea, but…
- It will never work
- It will cost too much to implement
- It will take too long to realize an ROI
- Why would we want to do that?
- Our existing customers don't want it
- We've never done it before

Good ideas do not necessarily sell themselves but need to be nurtured and marketed internally within an organization. Winston Churchill once said that "having a good idea is not the end; it's not the beginning of the end; it is the end of the beginning."

An age-old problem is how to create value from ideas and making it happen within an organization.

Re-thinking Assumpstions and Myths about Innovation

There's a temptation to see innovation as the fun side of business, the nice bits where you get to use your creativity (instead of all that execution stuff). Innovation though has to be rethought as a discipline that's distinct from cheer leading or brainstorming or crowd sourcing. So what are the top 4 assumptions we need to get rid of?

1. It's about creativity – recent research shows that creative people are the least likely to be seen as leadership material. If creativity is your bag, you are less likely to be perceived as a natural leader.

> **Reality**: it is about creativity but on a scale that opens up opportunities that we all need to grasp.

2. Innovation is about motivation – or you can cheerlead companies to success. A lot of innovation writing comes back to an over simplified belief that it all comes down to motivating people to get things done differently. But many of the critical innovations we need will – or will not – take place in companies of huge scale and complexity. Innovation is not so much about motivation and creativity as it is dependent on being able to scale new attitudes and also scale training.

> **Reality**: to get there we need a discipline called 'innovation management.'

3. Innovation is about the user, or the designer or being open, or any other single facet of change. For many of our most important organizations however innovation depends on being able to manage a matrix of factors all of which are changing. It is about users, designers, openness, social dynamics, ingenuity, the lab, and many other factors.

> **Reality**: the matrix of requirements means we need CIO's to work out what system or platforms will deliver on the management need.

4. Innovation is about building better products or services. In reality innovators fail 70 – 80% of the time. Innovation is really about how you manage the development and selection process through successive failures, which is often mundane.

Reality: There's no safe way to become a risk taker

I think we should treat innovation as a new management discipline, what do you think?

Myths That Inhibit Innovation

The first step on the way to inspiring innovation is to ruthlessly expunge the romantic myths that surround it — they often stop us from seeing the fresh ideas that are right in front of us. Here are four of the biggest myths about innovation, along with tips for seeing your way around them:

Myth #1: Innovation Involves Quantum Leaps.
According to this myth, innovation must be transformative. The PC was a quantum leap innovation, as were the printing press and the automobile. But there aren't many of these. Furthermore, quantum leaps typically involve high costs and huge risks. What might be a better alternative? Think constant, incremental improvement.

Myth #2: Only Geeks May Apply.
We're constantly told that engineers are the only people who make important innovations. But there are many other sources of ideas. Be open to all these sources. Innovators are people who pay attention, not just geeks cooped up in cubicles.

Myth #3: Innovation Requires Off-Sites with Geniuses.
Much has been written about Nathan Myhrvold's Intellectual Ventures, the company he started after retiring from Microsoft. He gets all his super-smart pals to read scientific papers and then convene to solve Big Problems. So far, they've filed over 500 patents — but where are the businesses? Ideas are cheap, functional

companies and real products are hard. Or, as Steve Jobs said, "real artists ship." Forget the geniuses; give thinking time to your staff instead.

Myth #4: Innovator's are a Special Breed
According to this myth, to be innovative, you need to hire an innovator with a track record. But beware: just like stocks, past performance is no guarantee for the future. Even Steven Spielberg has made flops. The romantic belief in the power of individual creative geniuses won't make you smart it will make you dependent. You'll do better to cultivate creativity as a process. Oh and by the way: your customers are fantastic sources of ideas, if you know how to talk to them.

If you work from the assumption that every person in your organization is capable of having a good idea, then you have to ask yourself a serious question: What is stopping that idea from contributing to your organization? It may be mythology. It may be processes. It may be individuals. It might even be you. What are you going to do about that? Where are your next innovations going to come from?

Innovation Killers to Avoid

A lot of things can go wrong on the long journey between the birth of an innovative idea and its actual implementation. Potential breakthroughs fail for many reasons, with even worthy concepts falling victim to the hazards of the development process, a situation that is all the more perilous in this era of stripped-to-the-bone budgets and thin staffs.

The pitfalls for innovation are more likely the result of bad planning than a lack of creativity. There can be a failure to appreciate communications skills, or confusion about what exactly innovation is. In the end, a successful outcome is as much about people as it is intellectual brilliance.

Here are eight innovation killers to avoid:

1. Rejecting Small Opportunities

   Any idea that furthers strategy can lead to valuable innovation.

2. Maintaining Familiar Metrics

   Standard operating procedure and routine schedules and budgeting won't work.

3. Rewarding Only Pre-Set Goals

   Innovation is about discovery along the way.

4. Sequestering Innovators

   The "I-team" must work with other departments to keep business goals in mind.

5. Not Leveraging Diversity

   Multiple talents and interests sharing a unified focus yield innovation.

6. Overemphasizing New Products and Capabilities

   Improvement of existing products and services matters too.

7. Ignoring Interpersonal Skills

   Smarts matter, but so does the ability to collaborate.

Avoiding innovation killers is essential. Have you identified any other innovation killers? Have you identified any techniques that keep innovation killers at bay?

The Quest for Innovation

Organizations express a desire to be innovative. It is the oft-cited statement from countless corporate leaders who evoke it in mission statements and look to it to drive growth. But like many corporate goals, innovation is often more a vague, conceptual symbol that a clearly define process. On closer examination, few organizations truly commit to innovation in a measurable way with head count, process management, or funding. Gartner research recently identified five myths that threaten to derail even the best-laid plans. They are:

1. Innovation just happens
2. Innovation only happens in R&D
3. The best innovation comes from inside
4. The more innovative ideas we generate, the better
5. We have lots of smart people, so innovating will be no problem

Dealing with the new economic normal of doing more with less, organizations need to offset the effects of this uncertain business environment and address these innovation myths. Think about it. R&D does not necessarily yield innovation as exhibiting by significant spending by pharmaceuticals and software companies. Contrast that to a breakthrough idea such as Facebook to see what can be accomplished on a limited budget. . It's important to recognize that R&D, product development, and innovation are radically different disciplines.

Innovation will require structure and planning focused at recovery, return to growth and the resolving of the organizations most critical challenges.

By addressing the myths about innovation and by developing a new model for leadership organizations will be better positioned to achieve these objectives.

Innovation outside of R&D in areas like process, service management and user interface that will increase the success rate and speed of new product, process and service development and deployment.

Organizations will continually look to outside collaborative innovations sources. Strong leadership will harness innovative technologies to drive deeper more meaningful business relationship. New business models will be developed that increase business flexibility and speed to market.

Creativity, Imagination and Curiosity

Creativity, imagination and curiosity go hand-in-hand to drive innovation. Consider that creativity is a skill set that employees bring. A 2008 study by The Conference Board, set out to understand how important "Creativity" is to today's business leaders. (Ready to Innovate) The survey results reflect employers' recognition that that creativity is of increasing importance in the workplace. In a 2010 survey (What Chief Executives Really Want, 2010) of 1,500 chief executives conducted by IBM's Institute for Business Value, CEOs were asked what key characteristics their business leaders will need to possess in the near future. This survey identified creativity as the most important leadership competency for the successful enterprise of the future. Until now creativity has generally been viewed as vital for R&D or product development, but not the essential leadership asset that must fill an organization. It's creativity—not operational effectiveness, skills, or even dedication.

Although they are invariably linked, creativity is not the basis for imagination. A way to differentiate them is to consider a flight to Mars as being imaginative but creativity is the STEM implemented approach to get there. The dictionary defines imagination as the ability to form ideas or images in the mind and the ability of the mind to be creative or solve problems. Imagination can help you see all existing possibilities and combine ideas and thoughts to improve upon existing strategies, business practices, or innovative new solutions. Some consider imagination to be the precursor to innovation. As Walt Disney once stated: "If you can dream it, you can do it. Always remember that this whole thing was started with a dream and a mouse."

Many innovators are simply curious people who are inquisitive, and like to solve problems. Curiosity is a key attribute of highly creative people. Leaders need to be inquisitive and cultivate curiosity within the ranks. They need to ask a lot of questions and challenge the norms or existing methods. Creativity and innovation don't happen if no one bothers to think of a question that needs answering. Creativity and innovation don't happen if no one bothers to think of a question that needs answering. Walt Disney once noted: "Around here, however, we don't look backwards for very long. We keep moving forward, opening up new doors and doing new things, because we're curious...and curiosity keeps leading us down new paths."

Curiosity has been the main driving force behind scientific activity. Curiosity can simply be defined as a desire to know or learn about something. It is an inborn part of life. Consider a toddler, we began to crawl and explore our respective surroundings. As we grew, we mixed curiosity with experimentation to learn about our surroundings. In some cases, curiosity fades with age but with others, the spark remains. Curious individuals are those that try the path not taken, take apart things and try to reassemble them, and don't sit idly by. Curiosity is the major driving force of creativity, learning, research and innovation. Without curiosity, people are indifferent or uninterested, which are emotions that don't really drive anything at all. Transformational leaders are risk-takers and encourage curiosity with their followers.

Albert Einstein once stated, "It is a miracle that curiosity survives formal education." Leaders need to embrace continuous learning that goes beyond any formal education or training that they may have had. Even if you are an expert in your field, you won't be for long if you don't continue learning. Become a voracious reader, not only in books that favor your interests, but those outside of your zone.

Scientific curiosity, insatiable in its explorations, does not know what it will find. NASA's flagship Mars Science Laboratory robotic rover was aptly named Curiosity in a worldwide content and public poll to name it. Curiosity's mission is to determine whether the Red Planet ever was, or is, habitable to microbial life. The rover, which is about the size of a compact car is equipped with 17 cameras and a robotic arm containing a suite of specialized tools and instruments. Teams at NASA and the Jet Propulsion Laboratory (JPL) have been sharing the historic moments of the continuing exploration activity on social media. The Mars Science Laboratory mission propelled the interest and attention of the nation back onto the space program. Interestingly enough, the Curiosity rover itself required innovation as it relied on a revolutionary new landing system that even the mission team conceded looked a bit "crazy".

Remember, "Millions saw the apple fall, but Newton was the one who asked why" ~ Bernard M. Baruch.

Innovation is grounded in curiosity. What are you curious about?

Chapter Three
Leadership Gap, Innovation Mandate

*Go as far as you can see; when you get
there you will be able to see farther*
—J.P. Morgan

A leadership gap is a shortfall between current and forecasted leadership capacity. Even though the term leadership gap has long been part of the business terminology, organizations continue to struggle with the important challenges of identifying, selecting, and developing leadership talent.

A leadership gap may have one of three causes: a leader may not be fully proficient in the required competencies; a leader that is not focused on the right skill areas; or the leader is simply over their head in their role for whatever reason. Unless rectified, these can have short or long term ramifications.

Organizations typically want innovation. However, innovation cannot be mandated, as it requires several key building blocks in order to succeed and flourish. These key areas include the internal business climate, resources, externals, corporate culture / values, and behaviors. An innovative climate cultivates enthusiasm, challenges people to take limited risks, fosters learning and encourages independent thinking.

In his book, Unrelenting Innovation: How to Build a Culture for Market Dominance, by Dr. Gerard J. Tellis, asserts that the single most important driver of innovation in any organization is its culture. He cites three organizational traits that are the key ingredients for innovation: "a willingness to cannibalize existing products, a risk-taking attitude and the ability to focus on the future". (Tellis, 2013) The concern that many companies have is the impact that the commercialization of innovations would have on the company's existing products.

The Wide Lens: A New Strategy for Innovation, by Ron Adner believes that that many products do not succeed or fail by themselves. Without either the proper support or complementary products or services, an innovation may not become commercially successful. He also believes that organizations focus on their own innovations but fail to recognize and leverage potentially complementary innovations that exist elsewhere in the eco-system. An example that Adner points to is invention of the electric light bulb. "The light bulb on its own was a miraculous invention but needed the development of the electric power network to turn it into a profitable innovation." (Adner, 2012)

Poor leadership can have serious ripple effects that impact the entire organization - from employee burnout to underperformance of the entire company. With global economic uncertainty and changing workforce, organizations face significant leadership challenges in the coming years.

The Innovation Buzzword

Everyone seems to be talking about innovation these days. How many companies can you name that state that innovation is part of their strategy and a central component of their future? They may have customer demonstration centers that tout innovation or have research teams or initiatives with the mantra to innovate. However, in most cases, innovation is no more than a buzzword and marketing catchphrase with very little actual change.

Consider the most noted example – The Xerox Palo Alto Research Center. Xerox assembled a team of world-class researchers in the information and physical sciences and gave them the mission to create 'the architecture of information'. Some of their innovations include the GUI (Graphical User Interface) which was the precursor to Apple's user interface and to Microsoft Windows, the WYSIWYG (What You See Is What You Get) text editor, bit mapped graphics, the Ethernet, the pioneering object-oriented Smalltalk programming language and the laser printer. While some of their research did advance Xerox's primary copier and printer product lines, Xerox has been criticized for failing to commercialize many of PARC's advances. According to those working at PARC at the time, the problem was that Xerox management was only interested in the PARC's research results that were directly involved with photocopiers.

The primary beneficiary of PARC's computer-related innovations was Apple Computer and their visionary co-founder Steve Jobs. Some of the basic ideas developed by PARC were enhanced and productized by Apple. Apple is a prime example of how innovation builds company value and brand equity to become one of the most valuable companies in the world with products that are sought after regardless of their price premium.

PARC continues today as a wholly owned subsidiary of Xerox and continues to innovate in a number of different business areas.

The Xerox PARC example may lead us to the conjecture that such separate labs or small research teams may are a mistake. Such teams may be disconnected from the realities of business, or become segregated fiefdoms that project to the organization that they alone are responsible for innovation and others 'need not apply'. What ultimately may work for a company depends on their corporate culture, strategy, and goals?

Innovation is not limited to the creation of a new product, service or something that comes out of an R&D lab. Innovation can be the combination of existing technologies or not rely on any technology. Innovation can also occur in the creation of or restructuring of business processes, marketing, or manufacturing techniques. Minimizing production cost means everything in manufacturing. This was the primary source of innovation for Henry Ford as he didn't invent the car but made a less expensive one by perfecting processes, such as the assembly line, that reduced the overall production cost.

People view and measure innovation differently

- New technology
- Better capabilities or functionality
- Lower energy costs
- Reduction of a carbon footprint
- Improved performance
- Use of renewable energy
- Improved ease of use
- Better quality
- New size
- Change in user behavior
- Convenience
- New or game-changing concept
- Improved social or personal well being
- Lower manufacturing / development costs
- Lower product or service cost

Innovation must ultimately have purpose for the organization such as:

- Creation of a unique business or being able to fulfill existing customer needs better
- Creation of new technology life cycles based on entirely new ideas
- Renewal a product life cycle or provide value added
- Improve internal business or manufacturing processes
- Improving customer responsiveness

All of these items have been used to describe innovation and its potential resultant output. The synthesis of what is required for innovation is captured in Figure 4.

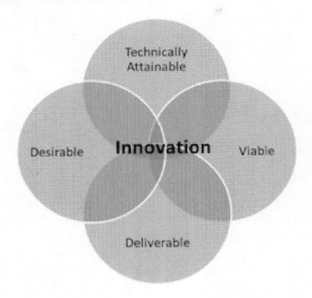

How Leaders Innovate

Although people sometimes have a flash of inspiration, most innovation requires funding and a plan to implement it. Innovation can be driven by awareness of an opportunity, a problem, a process need, or a technology. Once the need for innovation has been identified, convert it into a challenge that can spur dialog, invites creativity, and offers a positive spin.

There are two types of innovation. Most innovation is incremental, which is usually little more than the clever replication or reproduction of what were once breakthrough or disruptive innovations. Most innovation is of the incremental categories that come from small changes and in many cases are considered product innovations. This form of small incremental change is sometimes considered to be a form of a continuous improvement cycle that is meant to improve product or process efficiency and quality.

Innovation in the product or service domain is the result of finding new ways to solve the customer's problem that can benefit both the customer and the sponsoring organization. Innovation, in any form, can have a significant impact on an organizations ecosystem. Consider the areas potentially impacted:

- Employees
- Customers / End Users
- Supply chain / Distribution
- Marketing
- Operations
- Stakeholders / Stockholders

Given time, proper planning, and learning, any organization can improve its ability to cope with innovation.

An effective leader needs to correctly pitch a disruptive idea to the potential stakeholders and early adopters. There is the need to positively persuade this audience that the 'disruptive' change can deliver clear advantages to the potential user community. This requires a shift of focus from the need for disruptive change to the motivation for disruptive change.

From a leaders' perspective, consider the phases of an innovation as depicted in Figure 5. This Innovation Cycle represents a framework for classifying the different stages and stakeholders related to the development of innovation.

Innovation begins with noticing a problem or opportunity and contemplating a potential solution. Initially focus on the identification and introduction of your idea. This initial stage is the official birth of your disruptive idea. You must be passionate about selling your idea and persuade them to authentically believe in your vision. Consider how you speak and be sure to avoid techno-babble, jargons and slogans. Connect with everyone to ensure a comfort level and honest assessment about what you are trying to achieve. Explore and iterate your idea. Make sure that you don't get hung up by naysayers or stone wallers. For a disruptive idea to succeed requires its introduction to people who have the motivation to appreciate the change in status quo. You must listen to and work with your stakeholders to refine and tune it before taking it to the next level. Once your core group is sold on the idea, they will become advocates in helping to move it forward. This core group will now be your coalition. For ultimate plan execution and development, you may best pass those duties to other trusted and capable team members who fully believe in you strategic vision. A leader should be at the ready to maintain momentum and continuity. As more people get involved, optimize the solution. To communicate advantages, you should think about who would be eager to initially have and use your solution. The answer may be with the use of "early adopters." Continue brining more people into the fold and maintain a cheerleader status. Upon its ultimate launch, be there with your team. Upon its success, make sure that everyone involved gets the credit. A great leader never fails at innovation, learns from the experience, and doesn't pass along the blame.

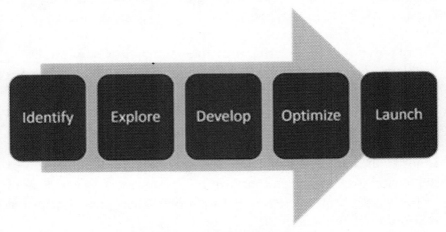

Innovation Phases

While most organizations do not have a clear strategy to innovate, here are some good examples of those that do:

- Google is a highly innovative company that has as one of its goals to invent the future. Google has diversified beyond its core search engine business with a multi-prong approach to reach this goal. First is through Google X, a secret skunk works lab whose most well known existing project is a self-driving car. These cars have already driven over 100,000 miles on public roads. Beyond this dedicated lab, Google engineers are encouraged to take 20 percent of their time to pursue new ideas with something that they are passionate about. Hit products, including Gmail and Google News, were created out of this program.

- Vanguard requires their employees to keep all their day-job responsibilities but can log extra hours to work on more cutting-edge projects with support of their management. Through this mechanism is akin to a startup venture, people bet their time and reputations on projects that may have impact on the business. Vanguard also has a mechanism and funding available for disruptive innovation projects.

Companies such as these have demonstrated that they can successfully and continually innovate in a repeatable fashion.

There are proven engineering principles and methods for attacking problems in need of innovative solutions. Companies need to turn the haphazard innovation process into a systematic set of processes, practices, and cultural changes. These processes need to be injected into the organizations complete ecosystem.

Innovation is not a one-time process. As James Allworth, Fellow at the Forum for Growth and Innovation at Harvard Business School (HBS) has written in his blog, the solution to disruptive innovation is continuous innovation. (Denning, 2012)

"Simplicity is the ultimate sophistication" is a quote attributed to Leonardo da Vinci. Simplicity should be the rallying cry for innovation. Ultimately innovative products should make products and processes simpler and easier. In the book, Insanely Simple: The Obsession That Drives Apple's Success, the author states that to Steve Jobs "Simplicity was a religion", and was his most powerful weapon that drove Apple to success. Consider the user interfaces and operation of Apple products. Jobs would obsess over the number of clicks that it would take perform an operation within an application. Apple designed complexity out of its products to make intuitive devices that anyone could easily use. Simplicity is a key part of its iPad, iPod and iPhone product lines. Simplicity was also critical for internal management processes and became a model for operational efficiency.

Would you choose complexity over simplicity for your products or business practices?

Innovation is directly proportional to the attitude and technical savvy of an organization's senior management. Even industry leaders can't always keep up with the latest technological advances. Faced with the prospect of falling behind the competition, larger companies sustain innovation through the identification and acquisition of small young companies along with their promising early-stage technologies in emerging markets.

- CISCO has become a role model for tech Mergers and Acquisitions (M&A) and an acquisition-as-growth strategy that substitutes for generic R&D innovations.
- IBM has undergone a large number of acquisitions during a corporate history along with a number of notable spinoffs (e.g., its venerable PC business to Lenovo and its printers to Lexmark).
- Apple has a clear strategy for making acquisitions as noted by Apple CEO Tim Cook. "If you look at the last three years, we've averaged an acquisition every other month," he said. "And the kind of companies we've purchased have been companies with really smart people and/or IP." As with most of their acquisitions, Apple takes the talent and

utilizes them based on their specific project needs. (Apples acquisition strategy, 2013) Some acquisitions can have a major long-term impact such as their acquisition of NeXT, developer of the OPENSTEP operating system, which now makes up the foundation of Apple's current Mac operating system.

Although this may be a viable approach to hedge against the possibility of missing out on a technological advance, the challenges of successful acquisitions are significant, as are the challenges of post-acquisition integration. And some M&A activity is related solely for increasing market share.

The important question is that do technology acquisitions facilitate innovation? A strategic management study by University of Pennsylvania, Wharton found that an innovation through acquisition strategy does not always pay off. Historical data shows that the majority of acquisitions fail. The study noted that failed acquisitions, tended to result from hasty purchases where the 'innovative' products that drove the acquisition were not functional or well understood, or information platforms between companies were incompatible. (The innovation through acquisition strategy: Why the payoff iisn't always there, 2005) Some notable success stores are from Apple, who built their iPhone/iPad ecosystem with a small number of judicious acquisitions and Google who created new ecosystems based on their purchase of Keyhole (which became Google Earth) and Android (which turned into a major Operating System).

These acquisitions must be brought in house with care to keep their innovative cultures intact. In a study by Emery University found that culture is critical to success in focused technology acquisitions. "A distinction is made between acquiring the relevant individuals possessing the appropriate knowledge and the role organizational culture plays in sustaining the contribution of that knowledge over time." (Abhishek Kathuria, 2011).

External to developing and furthering the innovation development to become something real, is its implementation phase. Depending on the type of innovation, this might mean market development, product sales, or implementation of the process. This is where ROI may ultimately be realized upon successful development and implementation. However, substantial investments may be required to reach this next step.

The Cost of Innovation

Most innovative ideas never reach critical mass. Innovation requires planning, perseverance, support, thought, and resources. The financial and resource implications of the wasted investment of money, time, and talent in pursuing the development of the idea can be significant. The amount of time that it takes to fully realize an innovation may however be its largest cost. The probable risks often negate such investments in the future. The costs of disruptive innovation, such as the development of a new drug (including the cost of failures) by the pharmaceutical industry, are 1.2 Billion dollars. (Innovation by the Numbers, n.d.)

It's expected that organizations have to do more with less. Organizations are now utilizing advanced innovative tools and processes to drive down the cost of innovation.

Examples of how innovation can drive innovation can be exhibited by the use of 3-D printing technology. This form of printing uses neither machining nor molds. The object is 'printed' or built from the bottom up by piling razor-thin layers of material on top of each other until a three-dimensional shape emerges. Rather than using custom machine tools to build early prototypes of new parts, the computer-guided 3-D printing technology is being used to design and test its engineers' latest ideas and refine them before being mass-produced. This new method allows product developers to have a prototype in their hands in as little as a week after they create a new design as compared to a three to four month time for conventional machine shops or injection-molding facilities. 3-D printers can produce a wide range of objects ranging from tiny nano-batteries to parts for a new automotive transmission. For example, Boeing has produced more than 20,000 3-D printed parts for its military and commercial aircraft including its new Boeing 787 Dreamliner. However, one of the most promising uses of this technology is in medicine. Some of the game-changing innovations currently being researched include entirely new artificial organs, artificial human skin, and custom prostheses.

Boeing, an icon of American innovation, has reshaped air travel over the past half-century. Let's consider the cost of innovation of the Boeing 787. It's a high tech marvel with a carbon-fiber composite body and a new electrical system that gives it reduced weight, which allows it to burn 20% less fuel than the comparable planes that it's meant to replace. But Boeing has been struggling to master these innovations that have significantly delayed delivery and raised costs. (Michaels, 2013)

While these are more radical forms of innovation, other incremental forms are happening through IT in the forms of cloud computing, big data, and enterprise mobility, which create new value through smarter technology.

The flip side to the cost of innovation is the missing cost of not innovating. This cost has been defined as the estimated dollar value your competitors have gained and that you have failed to achieve through your own efforts. Innovation requires curiosity and creativity but neither can be hurried. But how can you calculate the cost of not implementing and idea? Sometimes it is difficult to determine the value of creative and innovative ideas with its impact on the business. However, the ultimate cost of not implementing an idea can potentially be more costly such as in loss of market share by a more nimble competitor who followed through on a similar idea. History is littered with companies, which failed because they did not exploit innovative new ideas.

In their recent report From Overload to Impact: An Industry Scorecard on Big Data Business Challenges, it was found that 333 C-level executives from a variety of industries indicate that failure to adequately tap into their collected data is resulting in the loss of 10% of their average annual revenue, which adds up to an average loss of $40.8 million per year. (From Overload to Impact: An Industry Scorecard on Big Data Business Challenges, n.d.)

Too often short term financial performance goals drive an organization not to innovate.

Failure Fast

There are no points given for shots not taken. In other words, you can't succeed without first making an attempt. Also, using a farming analogy – seeds must be planted and nurtured within the proper climate to grow and prosper. Good innovation ideas, upon maturity, can be harvested to reap the benefits. Despite the best intentions, some percentage of the crops will not grow and will wither and die.

The development of a successful, innovative product can be expensive and fraught with risk. Just as companies must rapidly bring products to market, they must be adaptable to deal with failure in the marketplace, regardless of the reason why. Many failed innovations have strong financial support and attract the praise of both experts and consumers. The resulting costs of innovation failure have been estimated at $100 billion dollars for U.S. Fortune 500 companies, according to Anthony Ulwick, CEO of Strategyn, a San-Francisco-based innovation consultancy. (innovation failure probable and costly, n.d.)

Even such innovative companies as Apple and Google have had their celebrated failures. Apple's CEO had to issue a public apology for their significantly flawed mapping App, Apple Map, which replaced the first-rate Google App available on earlier iPhones. Google's Buzz never received any significant level of buzz from its users in the social media realm due to its late release. Organizations such as Google have the mantra or "Don't run from failure - Fail often, fail quickly, and learn". A noted example was the technological breakthrough analog video disc playback Selectavision system developed by RCA in which video and audio could be played back on a TV set using a special system similar to vinyl phonograph records. From its conception in 1964, until its product release in 1981, it fell victim to poor planning, internal management conflicts and technical difficulties that stalled its production by which time it was outmoded by the emerging Betamax and VHS videocassette formats, which additionally had recording capabilities. The associated advertising campaign was the most expensive project in the company's history. By 1986, RCA had discontinued the project, losing an estimated $600 million in the process, as sales were nowhere near projected estimates. Some claim that this crippled the company for its ultimate takeover by GE.

There are many reasons attempt at innovation fail. Consider the following steps that lead to better outcomes:

- Have a well-defined innovation strategy in place that aligns with business strategy.

- Have a collaborative and innovative team of individuals in place that can work through any internal barriers, gatekeepers and silos within the organization that will hinder the activity.

- Consider the use of idea management systems to structure and manage the innovation processes within an organization. Such tools are available from a number of vendors that facilitate a larger group of people to be involved in the overall process instead of limiting the activity to R&D or dedicated product development teams. These systems additionally allow collaboration among top management on strategies the team is developing.

- Spend on the "right" ideas that are in tune with business needs.

- Engage your best and most curious people on the project and give them enough room to breathe.

- Innovation is a large organization may require processes in place that resemble those of a startup.

- Take a page out of agile development methodologies by breaking down a potentially overwhelming goal into smaller progress goals. The concept of incremental progress and small wins maintains enthusiasm while reducing intimidation.

- Concentrate on really important creations and radical innovation.

- Have a "Plan B" in place if your idea does not evolve as planned. Can a portion of the idea be used elsewhere?

- The innovation team must be properly managed with a set of broad guidelines and objectives. An innovation project is generally more difficult to manage that a conventional project and there can be long periods of time in which little worthwhile appears to be happening.

- Having all relevant stakeholders involved in the process and everyone on board.

- Make sure that enough emphasis is placed on the ideas execution and not just the idea creation and generation. This can be characterized as the 'Ten Million Dollar' idea with the 'One Dollar' execution plan.

- Remote shortsighted leadership from the process and any management that is reluctant to push innovation and to stay in their comfort zone.

- What works on paper might not easily be transferred to an operational item. Prototype an operational version and test it!

- Ensure that management fully understands the complexity of the innovation and its full ramifications on the business. Management needs to be fully engaged in the innovation and what it brings.

- Consider any potential safety and environmental impacts to the innovation

- Consider external partners such as nimble entrepreneurial firms that can fill gaps with any shortfalls lacking in the team. University research can provide a potential low cost, high-value proposition.

- Perform a patent search to insure that your invention doesn't already exist.

- Maintain confidentiality and protect your IP and legal ownership rights.

- Consider crowdsouring as a mechanism to solve your problem but do so cautiously. Potentially only provide a small or discrete part of the problem through the crowdsourcing platform. Crowdsourcing is an open process that everyone – including your competition can see. Idea ownership rights may also come into question.

- Make sure that the adequate amount of funding and essential resources are provided

- The entire infrastructure must be considered with regards to the innovation and must be managed. Consider the invention of the light bulb. By itself, it was a disruptive innovation but it required a power generation infrastructure in the background to make it work.

Some important rules about failing.

- Small failures may be acceptable, as long as they lead to future success.

- Try to move failure to the beginning of the development process

- Be prepared for the numerous hurdles and dangers in the progression from idea and prototype to pilot to product rollout.

- Don't be risk adverse and stop at the first failure. In the period from 1878 to 1880 Edison and his associates worked on thousands of different theories to develop an efficient incandescent lamp before succeeding.

- Consider utilizing crowdsourcing as a mechanism to engage potential customers early in the process to gather their sentiment and feedback.

- Failures should be recognized positively. A fear which many individuals have in the development of a new idea is the social and psychological stigma of being associated with any failure and being considered 'a loser'. If someone is admonished for failing within a new idea, you can be sure that it will be the last new idea that you will receive from them. On being asked how he felt about repeatedly failing to design a working light bulb, Thomas Edison quipped, "I have not failed. I've just found 10,000 ways that won't work". Success only comes by trying often, failing often, rethinking, researching, and trying again. To alleviate fearing the consequences of failure, consider rewarded to team members through different incentives being monetary or "we tried and almost succeeded but learned something" awards, even upon failure. The mentality and focus of the team needs to change from winning to trying.

It's all about learning how to fail as quickly as possible.

Leadership and Innovation: The Monetizing of Good Ideas

To grow revenues and market share in the new world order, it's not only the survival of the fittest but also survival of the fastest. While good ideas and innovation are vital, innovation without agility could be an opportunity lost. It's easy to find inspiration, but you may also be on the lookout for ideas that not only interest you but you can monetize or develop into something profitable. Leaders understand that in order to stay healthy in an increasingly demanding marketplace, innovation must be a fully integrated part of their companies' business strategy. Innovations may range from small step-changes to large and utter breakthroughs. Successful organizations through smart leadership need to be able to inspire creativity and harness innovations through the organization and then speedily transition them to market. And that innovation must translate into a bump for the bottom line.

> "We look for opportunities where we can offer something better, fresher, and more valuable, and we seize them. We often move into areas where the customer has traditionally received a poor deal, and where the competition is complacent" —Richard Branson

> Whatever the mind of man can conceive and believe, it can achieve. Thoughts are things! And powerful things at that, when mixed with definiteness of purpose, and burning desire, can be translated into riches —Napoleon Hill

For every great idea that gets launched, many others more go the wayside because leaders simply don't know how to take action, aren't certain if it is something worth pursuing, or if the timing is right. Despite having great ideas, it's all about the execution.

There are several strategies that are vital to monetize ideas:

- For any new ideas to grow and thrive within an organization there must be a consensus amount the organizations leadership and management to first encourage innovation and then will allow innovation to flourish.

- You must have the dedicated resources and infrastructure necessary for ideas to prosper.

- Your company must have a creative process in place that is solely dedicated to the nurture of innovation and its implementation.

- Your organization must be able to deal with potential failure. Turn past failures into tomorrow's successes. Where there's failure, there's opportunity and the path to your next success. Thomas Edison took over 1000 tries to "innovate" a commercially available light bulb.

- Show creativity as a leader by trying new things, showing curiosity, and embarking on new adventures. Creativity is one of the most powerful capabilities that businesses leaders can have. A great leader can also unleash the organization's creativity and address the invisible barriers of corporate gravity. Note the statement from Steve Jobs: "The people who are crazy enough to think they can change the world, are the ones that actually do".

- Don't wait until you have all the details. The time it takes to become perfect an idea might be an assurance of missing an opportunity.

- Step out of the safe and familiar.

- Look at the big picture and make a plan. Being able to put your creative ideas into action is what separates wild ideas that go nowhere from wild ideas that pay off.

- Try to have a good understanding of your end users and answer all of the "W" questions pertaining to their product or service needs.

- Assess your brand. Is the strength of your name and renown sufficient to sell your product?

- Take a good look at your idea. How innovative is it and can it be considered Intellectual Property (IP) or proprietary?

- Consider patent monetization as an alternative. If the idea is patented, consider its commercial viability and its potential value. Is someone infringing the patent and how strong are the patent's claims? Does the patent cover the client's core or non-core technology? A company may be reluctant to launch a monetization campaign involving core patents for fear that competitors will fight back with counterclaims that would put its core businesses at risk.

- Consider the business aspects.

- What investment does the organization need to make in order to successfully fund the furtherance of the idea? What is the expected ROI and over what period of time? What are your financial targets?

Once all strategies are firmly in place, a leader can turn their attention and resources to transforming the incubated idea into revenue.

78 percent of executives who say that innovation is very important to their ability to succeed and strengthen competitive advantage in the next one to three years—according to the latest Global Executive Sentiment Survey by Insigniam. (Executive Sentiment Survey)

Business policies and practices should be created to spur innovation within the enterprise. Follow the example of Jeff Immelt, chairman and CEO of GE, who has mandated his divisional presidents to own the innovation agenda for their area of responsibility. Their compensation packages are tied to their ability to spur innovation inside their businesses.

Monetizing Intellectual Property

Good ideas can come in many forms. In the global economy, the knowledge component of products and services has increased dramatically in importance. This form of knowledge can be in the form of engineering design, formulas, and patents or other forms of Intellectual Property (IP). IP is the capital upon which digital age companies build their business on and is recognized as an important asset. It is considered as the foundation for market dominance and continuing profitability.

There are several monetization methods based on the organizations patent(s), financial goals, and strategic objectives that include:

- Direct Licensing whereby the organization retains ownership and management of the patent(s)
- Indirect Licensing whereby the organization transfers the patent(s) to a third party
- Enforcement of the patent under the credible threat of litigation
- Commercialization through the actual development of a product
- Direct sale of the patent

A patent monetization campaign can be costly for an organization. Evaluating a patent portfolio requires technical, business, and legal expertise.

Companies in many cases hoard this IP in an attempt to stop others from encroaching on their turf. In this new economy, it's the 21st century leaders who recognize the shift to knowledge as the primary source of value and can discovery and combine knowledge into new products and services faster than their competitors.

According to the IFI Claims Patent Services research, IBM racked up more U.S. patents than any other company for the 20th straight year with its 6,478 patents in 2012, marking a record for the company. South Korea's Samsung Electronics and Tokyo-based Canon ranked second and third. Google Inc. took a spot in the top 50 for the first time, with 15 more patents than Apple.
(IFI Claims Patent Services, 2013)

Some organizations stream of developed patents let companies produce a sizable revenue stream. For example, IBM's flow of patents produces about $1 billion a year in licensing revenue. The intellectual property also has the side benefits of the freedom to move into new businesses with less risk of being sued over technology. IBM also relies on its research centers around the globe as inventors outside of the United States according to Manny Schecter, IBM's chief patent counsel, produced about 30% of IBM's patents.

Companies like General Electric spent $4.6 billion in R&D in 2012. Since its inception, GE has filed over 37,000 patents in the United States and 1,652 in 2011. GE has developed much IP over the years. The problem is that GE has is that only a small number of those patents are turned into profits that help justify their R&D expenditures.

GE, has partnered with product development startup Quirky (www.quirky.com), to enable anyone to utilize and innovate on the mega-conglomerate's technology for new inventions. The Quirky community uses the concept of crowd sourcing that was previously discussed. Through the crowd-sourced community of inventors and entrepreneurs, GE hopes to turn the IP into commercialized products with any subsequent revenues split between GE, Quirky, and the inventor. Leaders should consider crowd sourcing as an alternative solution to solving their business problems. Companies such as Innocentive (www.innocentive.com) offer online platforms for crowd sourcing an organization's innovation problems to talented minds from all over the world competing to provide novel ideas and solutions.

Marketplace Value

Invention is accurately perceived as a cornerstone of innovation. It generates new ideas, patents, prototypes, designs, breakthrough experiments, and working models. However, it's innovation that transforms these inventions into commercial products, services, and businesses. Ultimately the marketplace only values an invention when customers use it or buy it. For example, the technology behind flat-screen TVs was invented decades ago. The breakthrough innovation was the application of that technology to the public's insatiable appetite for crystal-clear digital pictures on big-screen HDTV.

For the past 30 years, I have been teaching courses in the process of innovation in executive education programs and consulting with firms worldwide on the topic. When I started, the application of the word to new products and services was uncluttered by different interpretations or spin. But over time, marketers discovered "innovation." They found a word that evokes a good feeling without the burden of being specific. Do you want to avoid saying "new and improved"? Just say the product is the result of innovation. The word has come to mean just about anything that is new, which is too broad to be useful.

Competing with innovation for attention is invention, which is also surrounded by an aura of good feeling, conjuring up images of a computer being built in a garage and the inventor emerging as a billionaire folk hero. As a result, invention has been linked in the public mind to success in the marketplace, and that is not so.

When a new idea surfaces or a new patent is filed—that is an invention. It is the classic eureka moment when a person has an idea for the better mousetrap and sets about creating it, putting off concern about who will buy it for another day. At a different level, much of the basic research done in R&D labs in corporations and at universities is the invention process. It is research for the sake of building knowledge, which is certainly important, but not done with thought of commercialization.

Redrawing Social Boundaries

Innovation means the introduction of new technology that is exhibited through new products, services, or processes. These innovations are changing the way we see our world, and helping us find better ways to live in it.

There are numerous societal and economic challenges that the world is currently facing – such as the aging and health of the population, energy, and environmental issues. Society needs an association of academia, industry, and businesses to solve its global problems to move the frontier of science and technology forward with innovative solutions.

While innovation relies on scientific-technological progress, there are many societal interactions between various parties (businesses, researchers, entrepreneurs, end users, political decision-makers, government institutions, and the general public). Innovations and their resultant by-products require cooperation between the various entities as well as having to deal with economic conditions, cultural factors, societal acceptance and ethics. Both real and anticipated impacts of technology can become problematic at every single stage of innovation and technology development.

Consider communicating with our family, friends and work colleagues. A generation ago, it was by a landline telephone or hand-written letter correspondence through the Postal Service. Today, we're checking our e-mail accounts and social media networking sites, in addition to texting our friends, family and co-workers almost constantly. We've become glued to the mobile phone or portable computing device (i.e., tablet) and are constantly plugged-in both socially and to our work environment. We have migrated from the printed word to the written word to the technical word. Technological innovation allows these interactions to occur and has far reaching, both positive and negative societal impact.

At an antique store, I recently witnessed a mother showing her teen-age daughter an old-fashioned rotary dial phone and explaining how to use it. In another case, a friend was describing photography to his son and mentioned the limitations of a certain number of pictures to a roll of film and the need to have that film developed. Talk about quizzical looks. That is a significant societal shift in a single generation.

Customer demand and societal need are both tremendous drivers of innovation. The ability to satisfy an unmet need is the beginning of a successful business model. Therefore, identifying these needs is the critical leverage point that needs to be learned.

Responsible organizations should always consider the ramifications of commercializing their product or service and the potential fallout on other industries. Similarly leaders should not stick their heads in the sand and look to see what is happening around them and note the potential impact to their business.

As information is converted to digital form (e.g. voice and video), the ability to duplicate and distribute such information increases enormously under the auspices of the Internet and thumb drives. This has markedly changed both the book publishing industry and music recording industry. Consider the ownership and privacy associated with any digital content that has been uploaded to a third-party site. Do you read the license agreement when signing up for one of these services?

Consider the on-line open source encyclopedia Wikipedia. In addition to viewing its contents, anyone can be an editor or a commentator. People that have interest about a given subject can freely generate and share that knowledge.

There are cases where revolutionary technologies can redraw social boundaries. Examples of two such transformational innovations are the automobile and Google Glass.

Through the efforts of Henry Ford, he turned the automobile from an invention bought by the rich into a true innovation available to a wide audience that profoundly shaped the 20th century in many ways.

> "If I asked my customers what they wanted they'd have asked for a faster horse." —Henry Ford

Consider what the car has evolved to today with its plethora of features. Does your car come equipped with stability control, blind spot assistance sensors, or parking assistance? Then you're seeing the foundation that will eventually lead to fully autonomous vehicles. Now companies, led by Google, have made significant technological strides in making cars that drive themselves on public roads and in traffic. There are three states (California, Florida, and Nevada) that have legalized the use of self-driven cars for testing purposes. Insurance companies are involved in the innovation process around making cars safer. But while some technologies may reduce the likelihood of certain kinds of accidents, new risks are sometimes added. However, daunting legal, regulatory and cultural hurdles must be overcome before the cars are widely available to drivers.

Google Glass is the much-hyped wearable eyeglass frame computer that is currently under a limited beta release as a prototype. It features a voice-activated interface, Internet connectivity, and a small screen display which doesn't block out what's in front of the wearer while giving the ability to access and produce data. The device otherwise "augments" the user environment by adding a technological layer onto your surroundings offering the capability to look up or send information, provide directions, generate photos and video.

Inventor and futurist Ray Kurzwell believes that within five years, this type of computing visor device will become commonplace. An example that he gives is that when you see someone on the street, your visor will tell you their name and other pertinent information.

The business angle is significant based on the notion of a wearable computer that a person can use on a constant basis while both in motion and at rest poses some interesting and ominous concepts for advertising, as well as significant privacy concerns.

Society will need to come to grips with a different set of values, ethics and personal privacy issues. For example, Glass is seen as just another computer or recording device, neither of which are permitted in Las Vegas casinos. Others see Glass as a threat to drivers and want to ban its use on the roads.

As Google Glass transitions from a prototype experimental device to a full-fledged product, Google management must consider the tradeoffs of the potential market opportunity against the marketing and lobbying strategies required to permit its societal acceptance. While it may take a while for Google Glass to make inroads into the everyday person's life or solely remain a niche product for the geeks, innovative leaders should look forward to potential applicability to their business. For example, security organizations could use it to identify potential threats at public events; or health aid enhancements for people with vision or memory impairments.

All of these are examples of the social impact of disruptive technologies. Do any of your innovative solutions have any societal barriers?

Innovation using the "Freemium" Business Model

A recent study by Flurry Analytics found that mobile phone games that are free to download are actually making more money than those that charge. Rather than asking $0.99 to download a game you have never tried, these companies let you download the app for free, then entice their most avid players into paying quite a bit more than $0.99 for in-game virtual goodies like farm crops or power boosters. In June 2011, among the top 100 games, free games in the iTunes store generated nearly 2x as much revenue as games that charged to download.

Offering your innovative products and services for free, and charging your more committed customers for premium services, is actually a common strategy. This business model is often called "freemium," a term coined by Jarid Lukin and popularized by venture capitalist Fred Wilson.

The freemium business model works like this: Everyone gets your product or service for free, forever. But those customers who really like it, and find most value in it, will have a strong temptation to upgrade to a "premium" (paid) service which has lots of additional goodies. It is, at heart, a strategy of pricing by customer segmentation. I've developed some key considerations in developing and benefiting from the freemium model.

The freemium model requires that innovators rethink their customer equation. Acquisition (attracting customers) comes first, and monetization (turning them into revenue) is second. A freemium model adds value to your customer, by demonstrating the benefits of your service before they are expected to pay for it (a powerful incentive in this lean economy). It also adds value to your business in two ways:

1. Acquiring customers incredibly rapidly, with much less marketing spend
2. Monetizing your customers based on their price sensitivity, and the value they derive from your business. (Even your free customers may generate revenue via advertising)

Most importantly, a freemium model requires deep customer insight. It hinges on uncovering the key shift in behavior between your casual users, and those customers who truly value your service. What happens when customer love you? Do they use your service more hours each month? Use more data storage? Go on to advanced game levels? Use your product for work and not just personal use?

If you can find that customer insight, and if you can offer at least a basic version of your service at minimal cost to your firm, then you may be able to follow the freemium model, and make much more money by letting your customers in for free.

Leadership in Diversity Drives Innovation

Diversity should be a factor in leadership roles. Over the past several decades, businesses have become more inclusive of women and minorities, dismantling many of the traditional barriers to advancement. However blacks, Hispanics, and American Indians, who represent roughly 30 percent of the U.S. population fill only 3 percent of senior management positions at American corporations and nonprofits, according to Management Leadership for Tomorrow, a minority recruitment and development group. Women lead only15 Fortune 500 companies. Even fewer have black CEOs.

According to the book by Marie Wilson, Closing the Leadership Gap: Add Women, Change Everything, the title says it all. (Wilson, 2007)

A research study by the Catalyst Bottom Line Series shows that there is a connection between gender diversity on corporate boards and financial performance. For example, companies that achieve diversity in their management and on their corporate boards attain better financial results, on average, than other companies. (The bottom line: corporate performance and women's representation on boards, 2007) However, working mothers often face substantial odds in landing senior positions because family commitments can keep them from investing as much in their jobs as male colleagues or those women who return to work after taking time off to raise their children.

Gaining a quality STEM foundation, continuing beyond public education to any level from community college to Ph.D. can serve as the great equalizer and a means to propel diverse peoples forward.

Can't Have One without the Other

There is a huge role for leadership in creating and living a culture that values innovation. In this culture, innovation becomes everybody's job, with all brains engaged in the pursuit of what now and what's next.

So, the question is what must be present and valued in an organization in order to create this innovative culture?

Well, probably lots of things but here are four things at the top of my list:

1. Diversity - in every way that one human being is different from another.

   While our natural tendency is to gravitate towards those who are like us, innovation lies most often in unexplored places and with people who vary in thought, background, experience, gender, age, ethnicity and skill. The wider the net is cast, the greater the opportunity for innovation.

2. Relentless Change - as an accepted norm.

   Those who embrace innovation, also embrace change. They expect it. They create it. They even demand it. Innovation and change are inextricably linked. As the song goes, "you can't have one without the other"

3. Open communication - at all levels

   Innovation requires us to listen deeply, speak candidly, question constantly, challenge openly, and get a little messy in the process. In other words, an organization that values innovation will be light on bureaucracy and heavy on curiosity and transparency.

4. Failure - as a learning tool

   In order to break through the barriers of sameness and routine, we have to experiment and risk failure. Failure happens. In an innovative environment it is also expected because with each defeat we get closer to learning about what it will take to succeed.

So, what would you add to the list of must have leadership values for an innovative culture to thrive? How do you encourage innovation in your organization?

Secrets of Top Innovators

Top innovators consistently drive success via a number of key strategies that may not be oblivious. One measure of these companies is the industry standard of sales per square foot. Despite the fact that these companies represent a diverse sampling of industries — from gadgets to gold to golf shirts — almost all of them have woven their success from common innovation secrets. Here is the list of the top ten companies and their sales per square foot:

1. Apple: $5,626
2. Tiffany & Co.: $2,974
3. Coach: $1,820
4. Lululemon Athletica: $1,731
5. GameStop: $1,009
6. Costco Wholesale: $998
7. Signet Jewelers: $955
8. Polo Ralph Lauren: $904
9. Whole Foods Market: $867
10. Best Buy: $831

So what is it that these star performers are doing to put up such extraordinary numbers? They innovate by using one or more of the following secrets.

They turn "I want" into "I need": Other than Costco selling staple groceries, not one of these companies sells anything that anyone genuinely needs. But through a combination of drool-worthy products, exceptional merchandising, buzz, and fomenting what amounts to peer pressure among their target customers, these companies pull off masterful manipulations of customer psychology.

They aren't afraid of high prices: On the contrary, high prices are a key part of the formula for nearly all of these companies (Costco being the most notable exception). More expensive suggests better (even if it's not) and more exclusive (or elusive).

Costco has also become America's largest wholesaler by revenue and is stealing customers from other low-price rivals like Kmart, Target, and Wal-Mart. It follows a clear no-frills, low cost focus while collecting membership dues in the process. Sears was once a cost leader with a powerful mail-order business, until the concept of a big-box store emerged with the likes of Kmart. Even Best Buy, listed above, has been experiencing competitive pressures from its brick and mortar rivals as well as from new low cost Internet rivals like Amazon.com. Those businesses that don't keep their eye on the ball, find themselves losing market share.

They employ "strategic scarcity": It's hard-wired that one of the best ways to make someone want something is to tell him he can't have it. And many of these innovative companies use this secret, either in reality by controlling production (wait in line or you might not get one), or perception (only one purse in a heavenly-lit cubicle in a sparsely-stocked boutique). Both fuel rabid desire and support high prices.

Do you use these or other innovative secrets to drive business leadership? What ways are innovative strategies impacting your market?

Meeting a Need

Innovation is a very different concept. When a need is identified and a product or service is developed to meet that need, you have an innovation. People talk about the "invention" of the light bulb or the "invention" of the iPhone, when in fact neither Thomas Edison nor Steve Jobs were inventors. They both used existing technology in new ways with an eye toward a big market for the result. They were innovators.

This is not simply an exercise in definitions. Entrepreneurs work tirelessly to form and build businesses, and they need all the help they can get. When they are launching their first enterprise, it is important for them to understand that an invention, no matter how inspired, will not be worth much if nobody wants to buy it. For established businesses looking for new profit centers, it is important to understand that brainstorming new product ideas is worth far less than identifying consumer wants and needs and developing products or services to meet them. For policymakers trying to figure out how to support a region's entrepreneurial spirit, understanding the difference between invention and innovation can lead to distinctly different approaches.

My message for an inventor is to think more like an innovator. His or her success rate would almost certainly go up. I was talking recently with Michael Schuster, whose product, HydroRight, easily converts a standard household toilet into a dual flush system, using less water to flush liquids and more for a "full" flush. He told me that he had at least 60 good ideas for inventions, but he focused on HydroRight because it taps into people's wish to conserve water and it fulfills that wish for less than $20. Sales are skyrocketing at Home Depot (HD) and Amazon.com (AMZN). Sure, he has patents on the small inventions needed to create his innovation, but it is not the patents that are making money. It is widespread acceptance in the marketplace.

My message for those running established businesses, perhaps built on a single successful product and seeking to expand is to learn the innovation process. Spending time at the front end on what the marketplace needs, rather than trying to build a slick marketing campaign around a nifty invention that nobody cares about, is such a certain way to succeed that a business plan can include the guarantee of new revenue streams courtesy of innovation.

Chapter Four
Executing Leadership and Innovation

We must learn – individually and as
organizations – to welcome change and
innovation as vigorously as we have fought
for it in the past...the corporate capability
for change must be dramatically increased
　　　　　　　　　　　　　　　　—Tom Peters

What is the model for 21ˢᵗ century leadership?

Varied studies over the years have defined several key critical skills required for innovation leadership:

In a study of how leaders maintain their edge, an analysis by Forbes show at least three key things that the innovative companies do to create and sustain an innovation premium. The study noted that "how well companies leverage people, process, and philosophies (the 3Ps) differentiates the best in class from the next in class when it comes to keeping innovation alive and delivering an innovation premium year after year". (The World's Most Innovative Companies, 2012)

Innovation Culture

Corporate culture refers to "the shared values, attitudes, standards, and beliefs that characterize members of an organization and define its nature. Corporate culture is rooted in an organization's goals, strategies, structure, and approaches to labor. As such, it is an essential component in any business's ultimate success or failure". (answers.com/topic/corporate-culture) A corporate culture can be both formal (e.g., work/life policies) and informal (established workflows). A corporate culture may also evolve over time. Older organizations may be long established rules and stale management policies while newer entrepreneurial firms have a culture that thrives on agility and speed. The power of a corporate culture is sometimes not recognized by management.

A culture of innovation engages and challenges people to think independently, foster creativity and learning, and to take calculated risks. Innovation culture tolerates and learns from failure by realizing that for any success, there may be multiple disappointments and failures. For companies that originate a steady stream of new products, such as Apple, the focus on innovation has always been a fundamental part of the culture.

A poor innovation culture can result in increased personnel turnover, lack of marketplace competitiveness, and difficulty in retaining or hiring talented people.

Innovation Strategy

An innovation strategy can be defined as a plan made by an organization to encourage advancements in technology or services, usually by investing in research and development activities. The ultimate goal is the strategy involved in adding customer value and creating new markets. The strategic plan for an organization can range from

- Suggestion box / brainstorm – an organized system for idea submittal that can be viewed and judged by peers and/or management for ultimate disposition
- Continuous Improvement teams – a team approach to focus on incremental improvements as opposed to innovations. Sometimes referred to as Kaizen.

- New Venture / Greenfield teams – focus on innovations and potential breakthroughs
- Incubator labs / skunk works - well-funded advanced development teams that can develop tasks and innovations efficiently with nominal management limitations.

Innovation Governance

Innovation governance can be thought of as a system of mechanisms to align goals, allocate resources and assign decision-making authority for innovation, across the company and with external parties. (innovation management)

Innovation Leadership

According to venture capitalist, Henry Doss,"In today's world, leadership that is not innovative starts at the wrong end of the chain, the money and resources end. The thinking seems to be that you can innovate your way out of the dead-end paradigm of Labor + Capital -> Output by allocating more labor and more capital to a system or a problem." (Doss, 2013) The premise is that even with ideas, talented people, appropriate funding, etc., innovation leadership is required as the catalyst.

How to Innovate in the 21st Century

It has never been easier or cheaper to alter the direction of a business, and companies that don't lead and innovate in response to changing market conditions may not survive at all. In an economic downturn, innovation isn't your best friend; it's your only friend. You don't need to be Steve Jobs to come up with a novel business idea. Nor is innovation all about high-tech inventions or new products. As many successful leaders will tell you, incremental ideas can be just as important as breakthroughs.

But how do you find that clear, purposeful frame of mind amid the pressures of modern business life? What makes for an innovative company? How much should owners listen to their employees? Is there an ideal company size for generating good ideas? Does time off get the juices flowing?

Here are some tips from the trenches of modern leaders and innovators.

STEP 1: Look behind you

> History can be a great teacher. Try looking back to see what did and did not work. Before you set out to change an industry, know its history.

STEP 2: Lose the routine

> Make time to read widely, and cultivate a variety of friends and online groups who send you wacky articles. Jump out of your rut by hitting a trade show or attending a seminar about an unrelated industry. Also try spending a day in the life of your client.

STEP 3: Use the brains you hired

> Smart leaders maximize innovation by encouraging everyone to think innovatively about the business. Target diversity. One of the simplest way to help a company think outside the box, is to bring in people who have lived in different boxes.

STEP 4: Get cozy with customers

> You can't be too close to your customers. Your customers are your lifeblood. Understanding your customers' problems and how to solve them is the heart of innovation. It's easy to get in a rut with conventional wisdom. Innovative thinking from outside your company challenges the status quo.

STEP 5: Try to fail quickly

> Put enough energy into the innovative idea to determine its value. Constantly fail forward by learning from quick failures and driving toward strategic leadership and innovation.

Have you found any other methods that accelerate innovation??

Innovation Leadership, a Matter of Behavior

A recent innovation leadership carried out jointly by IESE Business School and Capgemini Consulting suggests there are five key areas that affect a company's innovation success: the innovation function, innovation strategy and innovation governance (formal mechanisms), innovation leadership and innovation culture (informal mechanisms).

The study notes specific differences in behavior of innovation leaders versus laggards across these key areas. The behavior of leaders has an impact in the ability to drive innovation.

Additionally critical to innovation success is the development of a well-articulated innovation strategy. The lack of such a strategy is by far the most important constraint for companies to reach their innovation targets, followed by a lack of understanding of the external environment. There is a need for innovation strategy development in a more bottom-up manner, focused on people as the key source of competitive advantage. One needs to capture all those individual insights from managers and employees to better incorporate an understanding of the external environment in the strategy development process.

Have you developed an innovation strategy and are you achieving success with it?

Critical skills

There are numerous leadership skills and abilities that are valued in leaders today. Here is a compendium of leadership traits that you should be focused on to improve personal and business performance.

1. Self-Knowledge

In their book, Leading with Conviction: Mastering the Nine Critical Pillars of Integrated Leadership, authors Shalom Saar and Michael Hargrove (Shalom Saar, 2012) believe that self-knowledge is a key prerequisite for effective leadership. " It allows us to trust our instincts and to step back, reflect, and act from a place of considered conviction. And it ensures that our actions, although adapted to each specific situation, will be consistent and ring true. If we've made the effort to understand and cultivate our natural response to crises, for example, we are better positioned to take the lead in a situation of extraordinary organizational stress. Others immediately sense and are inspired by our calm authority". "Understanding ourselves allows us to leverage our strengths and manage our weaknesses. When we truly know ourselves, our personal difficulties and even our failures can become assets. Meeting difficult challenges provide essential learning experiences that fuel our determination to succeed and provide a foundation for future positive outcomes".

2. Vision

   A true leader needs to define the organization's future direction and to maintain it through any unanticipated problems that may occur. Craft a vision and drive forward.

3. Listening and Communication

   Leaders need to clearly, concisely, and powerfully communicate their vision, both in written and oral forms.. A leader must actively listen to and actively hear all points of view to make informed decisions whether they agree or not. Though a person might be a leader, that person will never treat others as beneath them and considered as their equal.

4. Respect, Motivation, and Team Building

   While communication is a key attribute, it is also about inspiring others and stimulating people with the established vision and goals for the organization. A leader values and engages others. Leaders must not only energize and invigorate employees about the type of work to be done as opposed to forcing "their way" down an employee's throat. A leader must understand differing opinions in the workplace and show respect all of their co-workers and not patronize them. Differing opinions are sometimes the spark of innovation. They build a strong team of competent, knowledgeable, and supportive people by getting the most from each team member.

5. Life-long Learning

    Leaders are willing to learn. Leaders need to commit to continue in furthering their own knowledge through self-learning, formalized training and mentorships. Learning about the organization and problems at hand in order to make the correct decisions additionally builds courage. They also need to make sure that their workforce is well trained. According to Former Great Britain Prime Minister, Benjamin Disraeli, "Seeing much, suffering much, and studying much, are the three pillars of learning".

6. Passion, Focus and Attitude

    Show passion in everything that you do and maintain a positive and optimistic attitude despite any negative situation that might arise. This involves knowing who you are, what you believe in, and where you are going. Stress common values in the team and enlist them in a mission to follow the established vision and direction.

7. Innovation and Change

    Continuously come up with new ideas and implementing them. This may involve stepping "out of the box" to explore new ideas outside of your comfort zone. Leaders should relish change and consider it as an opportunity as opposed to it being a threat.

8. Agility, Speed and Flexibility

Break down organizational barriers and the nonsense of bureaucracy that can be derived from focusing on organizational speed and agility. Be a critical thinker and rapidly assess core issues of situations to rapidly decide on the appropriate course of action. Be able to adapt quickly to new and evolving situations.

9. Courage

A leader needs to believe in their own humility, constantly grow from a continuum of experiences, and always be guided by their own instincts and values. Make tough decisions, knowing that bad decisions will be penalized. Remember that doing nothing is always an option.

10. Networking

Leadership networking is about building relationships and making alliances in service of your organization. Networking is an integral part of your role as a leader that helps you develop and nurture related skills that can you create benefits for yourself and your organization. True networking should go beyond use of social sites such as Facebook and LinkedIn. According to Curt Grayson, author of Leadership Networking: Connect, Collaborate, Create, "It goes beyond knowing or linking to lots of different people. It is about being able to use those connections wisely to solve problems and create opportunities." "If you have a great reputation within your network, you have the advantage of having a solid group of contacts who can be resources if you start a job search or look to extend your professional reach," adds Grayson.

11. Collaborations and Partnerships

Collaborations between industry and academia are promoted by open innovation programs, which have become a model for R&D. These innovation models can be based on face-to-face, side-by-side collaborations with common shared resources or separate facilities with well-coordinated activities. Corporate-academic alliances can through an on-campus presence be very beneficial to a corporate partner through its access and attraction to the best and brightest students for potential future employment. This close relationship can also provide a valuable resource for new ideas and perspectives that may not be prevalent in a business environment. Partnerships between industries can be a viable option. A partnership is an opportunity to leverage skills and capabilities that one organization may not have and ultimately offer a better end result product or service.

12. Diversity

Diversity goes beyond simply a matter of creating a heterogeneous workforce. Utilize the best of a diverse team to fully harness the power of diversity. A leader should challenge people from different cultures and disciplines to achieve creative breakthroughs.

Business leadership skills cannot be acquired by reading about it, as it requires lots of consistent practice. "Leaders are made, they are not born. They are made by hard effort, which is the price which all of us must pay to achieve any goal that is worthwhile." —Vince Lombardi

How do you measure up? What skills can you add to this list?

Habits of innovative, high-performance companies

Today's thinner revenue streams, narrower margins, heightened competition, and more limited resources have, if anything, increased the already high levels of stress among corporate survivors and raised the performance bar set by business executives. That has prompted changes in the ways companies invest, manage, and innovate—changes designed to minimize risk.

In a survey involving more than 280 product executives in 17 different industries, common patterns emerged among the study's top performers. Among the good management habits of innovative, high-performance companies:

- Balance. Investments in breakthrough advancements were offset with spending on incremental innovations. While the rewards of home-run products are potentially very high, their associated risks are even higher. Winning companies don't bet all their chips on blue-sky projects.

- Prioritize. Focus on product development projects that align with both market needs and the company's overall business strategy. Struggling to satisfy customer desires is only beneficial when it advances your company's longer-range objectives.

- Analyze. Overcome the largest risk in product innovation— products that customers won't buy—by analyzing customer feedback quickly to ensure delivery of products the market is actually asking for. If a product idea is going to fail, or meet only 80 percent of customer expectations, it is a huge advantage to find that out as soon as possible, drop the idea, and move on to other, more appealing projects.

- Automate. Top performers delivered products on time by using technology to manage requirements, administer workflow, and prioritize development. Too many companies rely on slower, less reliable manual processes.

There was also a flip side to the study's findings: challenges that consistently elude companies that are still struggling. Chief among them:

- Not listening. Listen to and consider the expressed needs of customers. Those diverse voices must be considered, reconciled, and balanced to develop a truly successful product.

- Not collaborating. Failing to share information and collaborate with customers, partners, suppliers, and other key stakeholders in exploring new ideas. For struggling companies, fewer than half their product ideas came from these sources.

- Misalignment. Too often senior management and product-line staff fail to communicate, which often results in their spending time and money on the wrong product priorities.

- Uncertainty. The lack of clear decision-making and confusion over product-line ownership leads to decisions based on internal politics, subjectivity, personal influence, and debate skills rather than product merits.

- Paperwork. Paper-based methods and other traditional innovation management processes slow down the development life cycle, especially for complex products.

- Poor execution. Struggling companies have trouble planning the resources needed to match market opportunities, difficulty managing multiple teams and regions, and a hard time managing the risks associated with new and existing products.

There are concrete steps that struggling companies can take to redirect themselves along the road to success, as well as steps that currently high-performing companies can take to reach even higher levels. Key among them: collaborate closely with key stakeholders, harness the wisdom of crowds, clearly define and convey product requirements, leverage outside help, and automate the innovation process.

What attributes do you think make for an innovative high performing company?

Three Practical Ways to Become an Innovative Leader

Innovation doesn't require genius, luck, or magic--but it does require talking to the right people, being able to clearly articulate a vision, and putting the right partnerships in place. Having a practical guide can help anyone develop into an innovative leader. Here are my top three steps:

Step #1. Talk to the Right People
Your most important asset is your mind. Your experience, expertise, and know-how governs your understanding of what is possible, the options you see, the strategy you formulate, and your assessments of the environment around you. To expand your vision, meet with other minds! Make it a habit to identify and visit the people who will provide you with fresh ideas, key learning, new tactics, and strong strategies.

Step #2. Articulate the Way Forward
People rely on their leaders to craft a vision of the future that makes sense and can guide their everyday decisions. Some of the leaders I have met improvise this activity and many do it badly. And yet articulating a rousing vision of the future isn't difficult. It can be your secret super-power, if you just master three tactics:

Be explicit about your conclusions and how you came to them. Speak in terms people can understand and relate to. Do more than share judgment--provide insight to your reasoning.

Give people the opportunity to ask questions. Encourage diverse points of view and different backgrounds. Let people react, inquire, challenge, and extract the information they need to satisfy their understanding. Then you will be in the best position to move forward together.

Customize your message to your audience. Include something useful in their day-to-day work--utility helps information stick.

Step #3. Build Informal Partnerships that Generate Synergy
Leadership today is largely about identifying the partnerships that will lead to broad, powerful impact and growth. I'm talking about supportive and symbiotic relationships here, not contractual business partnerships.

Some many leaders shy away from informal partnerships, fearing the vulnerability that comes with relationships. If you overcome that fear, you get the benefits. Here are tips to help you master the third step of innovation leaders:

Be clear about what you hope to get out of the partnership. Take the time to articulate the value to both parties that makes it worth pursuing.

Share the goals of the partnership with others who have a stake in its success. Initiate informal conversations, over the phone, via email, or over coffee, with the clients, vendors, industry experts, investors, and others who can share their perspectives how to get the most out of your partnership. Then share what you learn with your partners.

Take the lead in coordinating partnership activities. Be the one who identifies and handles important issues as they arise. Take responsibility for planning and facilitating joint events. Foster joint development. Provide regular assessment of the partnership that proves its value.

1+1+1 = > Sum
These three tasks required of innovative leaders--talking to the right people, articulating the way forward, and building informal partnerships--work together. The interaction of these contributions produces a total effect that is greater than the sum of the individual components. Together they ensure your leadership is well informed,

a source of unambiguous guidance, and reinforced by powerful allies.

Are you using these steps to become an innovative leader? What steps do you find most successful?

Flexible Leadership Driven by the 3C's

It's often not what a leader does but rather how they do it that makes the most impact. While some are, take charge in your face and others are content to play an off-stage role and work behind the scenes, all 21st Century Leaders should be driven by the 3Cs: context, circumstance and consequence. Leaders need to be flexible and apply a leadership style that fits the situation. Considering context, circumstance and consequence is a good way for a leader to determine how involved to be and what style to employ. Here are some guidelines:

- Figure out the context. Leaders need to know the back-story, that is, what happened before they arrived on the scene. Sometimes it requires digging and asking lots of questions. For leaders of long tenure, knowing the context is second nature. They live it every day. Knowledge of the situation and its context sets the stage for what the leader does next.

- Circumstance – the current situation–determines your degree of involvement. Crisis calls for bold actions. For example, if a new marketing program fails to generate sufficient awareness, the chief marketing officer should handle the situation. If multiple marketing initiatives fail, the leader needs to find a solution quickly. He or she should take charge and find a new senior marketing executive.

- Consequence is what happens when a leader acts. With apologies to Sir Isaac Newton, every leadership action does not have an equal and opposite reaction. Very often a

Leader's decision is designed to turn the enterprise around or keep it on course; a front-line manager's decisions are the equivalent of trimming the sails. A Leader who makes too many decisions not only creates lots of activity, specifically churn, they can also undermine the authority of other senior leaders.

Employing a style or knowing how and when to get involved comes with experience. New leaders are eager to put their stamp on their tenure and often unloose a bundle of initiatives. Too often many fail because the organization was unprepared, or more precisely the context and circumstance were not right. Getting the balance – hands on versus hands off – right does not come overnight but by paying attention to context, circumstance and consequence a leader can learn to get it right.

How have you found the right balance? Have you successfully used the 3C's in attaining flexible leadership?

Moving to the C-Suite Requires Development of these 3 Skills

A new generation of top execs has come into power over the last few years that don't look much like their predecessors, at least in terms of skills. They aren't necessarily the most technically brilliant at preparing a forecast, nor are they Zen masters of the supply chain.

Sure, those capabilities helped them rise up in the organization, but it's not what got them to the C-suite, according to an article in the March issue of Harvard Business Review. What skills need to be in your toolbox to make it to the very top?

Soft skills
"Technical skills are merely a starting point, the bare minimum," write authors Boris Groysberg, L. Kevin Kelly, and Bryan MacDonald in The New Path to the C-Suite. "To thrive as a

C-level executive, an individual needs to be a good communicator, a collaborator, and a strategic thinker — and we think the trend toward a general business orientation over a functional orientation will continue." (Boris Groysberg, 2013)

Relying on interviews and examination of hundreds of executive profiles developed by the executive search firm Heidrick & Struggles, the authors lay out the new job requirements for seven positions: CIO, chief marketing and sales officer, CFO, general counsel, chief supply-chain-management officer, chief human resource officer, and CEO.

For example, here are the new requirements to take the chief information officer position in your firm:

- Ability to view the business holistically, across functional, unit, and regional boundaries
- Process orientation and comfort with organizational design
- Information analytic knowledge; ability to help companies sort through and use information
- Expertise in investment allocation and using ROI to make decisions about future IT expenditures

Are these three skills in demand and recognized as critical to reach the top in your organization? What are other skills that you see as important?

Leadership 101: Managing Up

Learning to manage up is required if you want to succeed in corporate America. It's as important as getting the job done. Managing up gives your leaders a way to see the work you do in a way that will benefit you. It also creates job security. Here are five ways to manage up that will put you in line for raises, security, and a fulfilling career.

1. Don't blame your boss for anything. There is no point. Your boss is in charge and you are not. Make a note of what annoys you and tell yourself you won't do it when you are boss. (Although beware, there are no perfect bosses. Just like parenting, you will suck as a manager in your own special way.) When you manage up properly you will be able to turn your bad boss into a good boss. You can work around your boss's foibles if you stay focused on your goals.

2. Don't wait for your performance review to fight for a raise. Find out the salary politics way before your performance review. What's your boss up against when it comes to approving a raise for you? What do you need to do for him to help? Who are the influencers? Start managing all of them. Your salary review will need to be approved by a bunch of people. Make sure they love you BEFORE performance review time. By the time approvals come around, it's too late to ingratiate yourself. And, if it should come down to your boss really having no power over the purse strings, ask for non-financial compensation, like conferences and gadgets or whatever it important to you.

3. Find out what your boss is being measured on. Your boss definitely cares more about his own salary review than about yours. The more you help your boss to meet his goals, the more likely he is to go to bat for you to meet your own goals. If you do lots of work but it's all outside the parameters of your boss's goals, your boss won't notice. Do the work that matters, and then translate that strong performance into action from your boss. This means that the person who puts their head down and gets all their work done perfectly is not smart. There is no point in being the hardest worker in the office because all work is not equal. The work that is important is the work that gets noticed. Do less work so you have more time to understand what work matters.

4. Get benchmarks early, but be open to them changing. Your boss just wants you to make a difference on the team. He doesn't really care about your performance goals, per se. He cares about his own, his teams, and your participation to meet those goals. So help your boss to keep track of you by shifting your goals to be in sync with the company's goals. Your boss will be surprisingly open to shifting goals in the name of helping the company. And you'll find that shifting makes you look more like a team player, and like your irreplaceable to your boss.

5. Be nice. Really, there is no better way to ensure a good performance review if you are well liked by your boss. People get hired for hard skills to get the job. But they get fired and promoted because of their soft skills that make people like them. So really, the performance review is a great time to solidify your relationship with your boss after a year of hard work creating that relationship.

Chapter Five
Mentorship and Coaching

If your actions inspire others to
dream more, learn more, do more and
become more, you are a leader
                                    —John Quincy Adams

Mentorship and coaching can have great impact in the success of a 21st century leader, There is the vital need to capture and retain the institutional knowledge gained and lessons learned through its series of successes and failures and pass this knowledge along to prepare the next generation of leadership. The impending retirement of the baby boom generation has further elevated the importance in furthering the development of the next generation of leaders through mentorship and coaching.

During the industrial age, the path to a gainful employment often required apprenticeships and on-the-job mentoring. There was no other option to either learn a trade or to master a particular craft but from someone that was already in that profession. In many cases, this was a direct one-on-one learning process. In the 21st century, this master / apprentice process has evolved to that of the modern mentorship process but less upon passing along basic skills to that about passing along experiences and guiding ones students' career path.

Not so long ago, it was customary to rely upon personal real-time communications with our friends or peers that in many cases was dictated by geography. Technology both limits and enhances communication. In our globalized world, we are distancing ourselves from that personal level of communications through the use of cell phones and emails. Additionally there are new levels of contacts and potential sources of information now available through social media connections and the ubiquitous Internet with its dearth of information have all had an impact on the state of mentorships. Reaching out to ask an experienced person a question or to follow a blog post or Tweets lacks the personal relationship and relationship of trust required for a successful mentoring experience. Mentoring or networking isn't about how many people you follow or how many people follow you.

A successful mentoring program requires the following:

- Mandated Participation by both the mentor and the mentee with committed times by both parties
- Establish a personal relationship and bond of trust
- Establish a comfortable and preferred communications vehicle such as face-to-face, phone, email, blog or tweet. While personal face-to-face mentoring has its benefits, it is not always possible or practical. The digital era now allows for multiple channels for mentorship.
- Set expectations as to the scope of the interactions
- Follow through with regularly scheduled meetings to insure rapid information exchanges
- Provide good examples and guidance.
- Offer personal and leadership experiences
- Use the theory of reciprocity whereby mentors control the flow and direction of the conversation by the rate at which the information is revealed.
- Maintain a two-way conversation to exchange ideas with those that are mentoring us. Are you willing to both educate and learn from your interns?
- Establishing a network of mentors that forms a group of trusted advisors and beneficial relationships

The role of the mentor is to capture the lessons learned and experiences gained in order to prepare the next generation of innovation leaders. The importance of mentorship and coaching for innovation leaders should not be neglected, as it will make them more effective and efficient in their work.

Another form of mentorship is reaching out to the community at large to bestow our own knowledge and experiences onto others. This can be reaching out to local schools or the university community to

- Offer internships or after-school programs
- Participate in training programs to help others benefit from your experience
- Participate in STEM activities to help motivate youth

Picking a Business Coach, Learn from Other Exec's

Have you ever considered getting a business coach? Apple's Steve Jobs and Google's Eric Schmidt are archrivals in the mobile phone business, yet they share at least one thing in common. They both rely on Bill Campbell as a mentor and business coach. Campbell is the former CEO of Intuit (now chairman of the board) and he did exactly what Jobs and Schmidt are trying to do; build a publicly traded consumer-oriented technology company.

So how do you find a mentor and business coach? The key is to find someone who has done what you are attempting to do. Like Steve Jobs, Bill Campbell had led a company in which engineers wanted to make things complex while customers preferred easy-to-use products. Campbell successfully balanced those two interests at Intuit and therefore makes a good coach for Jobs. Eric Schmidt led Google from entrepreneurial leadership under Sergy Brin and Larry Page to an era of professional management while Brin and Page were still in the building. Likewise Campbell led Intuit while founder Scott Cook was still actively involved in the company.

Campbell found a way to involve Cook without undermining his own authority to lead. Therefore Schmidt made a good choice in selecting Campbell as his coach.

Who is your mentor or business coach and how did you select them?

Can your perfect Mentor find you?

The advice has become almost a cliché: Find a mentor who can help you speed-learn the lessons needed to advance your career — a Yoda to instruct young Luke in the ways of the Jedi. This is bad advice. Yes, mentors can help dramatically. But you can't find them, they need to find you.

Harvard Business School professor Linda Hill calls it the "myth of the perfect mentor." In this recent interview on The Root with Harvard professor Henry Louis Gates, Jr. she explains: "When my MBA students come up to me and say, 'Professor Hill, when I get to work I'm going to find a mentor, and he or she will do X, Y and Z for me.' And I say, 'Why would anyone do that? They are already paying you."

Instead, she says, learn to be the "perfect protégé," a person that others are attracted to and want to mentor. A perfect protégé, for example, knows the value of listening over talking. "One of the things you need to be able to do is take negative feedback, because we can only learn if we get feedback from other people," she tells Gates. If you bristle at criticism, teachers won't want to teach you.

In her classic Harvard Business School paper from 1991, Beyond the Myth of the Perfect Mentor, she offers several ideas on mentoring that remain extremely relevant today.

Think mentors, not mentor. "All work relationships should be understood as potential resources by which developmental needs can be addressed," Hill wrote 20 years ago. There is likely no one single person that can help you at all stages of your career. Typical mentor-protégé relationships last from two to five years.

It's not just about career. Some mentors can help you advance your career by introducing you to the right people or by acting as a buffer. But you also need psychosocial tutoring—enhancement of one's sense of competence and effectiveness in a professional role.

Consider development when evaluating job choices. "Seek out those positions and organizations that provide a supportive context for establishing developmental relationships," Hill writes. "For women and minorities, it is important to be aware of the number of individuals like you in the organization, for that number will have an impact on the availability and character of developmental relationships."

HR and Leadership Development

According to the 2012 Society for Human Resource Management ((SHRM) survey, "Challenges Facing HR Over the Next 10 Years," the number two HR concern for 52 percent of respondents is developing leaders. This is a big jump from the 2010 survey, in which a mere 29 percent of respondents named leadership development a pressing HR challenge. In business, as in the rest of life, leadership skills are critical now more than ever.

The number one spot in the SHRM survey with 60 percent of respondents is 'retaining and rewarding the best employees'. This makes sense as a lead-in, since I'd argue the best employees are leaders – people leaders, management leaders, creative leaders, technical leaders or sales leaders. We need to fill the leadership gap, and fast.

Here are the top four challenges to developing leaders and a bit about how to address them.

1. Invest in leadership development. Whether you believe leaders are born or made, companies still need to invest in their best employees to develop and sustain leadership qualities.

2. Create a culture of collaboration. Leaders are at their best when the company culture demands collaboration. Rewarding individual success is necessary but not sufficient.

3. Develop communications skills. We may expect our leaders to be good communicators but too often it's not the case. Good communicators build teams and trust; poor communicators create and feed uncertainty.

4. Drive and sustain real accountability. Leaders must be accountable. They must own the problems they need to solve and own their failures to be credible when claiming success.

HR and leaders alike have many responsibilities. Maybe among the most important is developing the next generation of leaders and being more innovative as times change rapidly before our eyes. Where would you start?

Part 2:
Innovate via Disruptive Technologies

*Never innovate to compete, innovate
to change the rules of the game*

—David O. Adeife

Chapter Six
Disruptive Innovative Technologies

Innovation distinguishes between
a leader and a follower

—Steve Jobs

The resultant outcome of technologies is expected to in some form improve the quality of our lives. There are numerous technologies that we can all point to that have had an impact on our lives and it is difficult to imagine any aspect of an organization that hasn't been touched by it in some way. If asked, most people will point to current technologies such as iPhones or a social media app that has changed how we live or work. While these may be important parts of our lives today, they can't compare to innovations and technologies that are truly impactful in how they have transformed society.

An early example of such a technology would be the invention of the movable type printing press as it opened up access to written communication and the global sharing of knowledge. His invention allowed for the mass production of printed books whose publication became economically viable for printers and readers alike. It played a key role in the development of the Renaissance, Reformation, the Age of Enlightenment, and the Scientific Revolution. About 500 years later, a more modern technology would be the development of the Transmission Control Protocol/Internet Protocol (TCP/IP) networking laid the foundation for distributed computing and the Internet.

The impactful technologies of history are those that have changed how we do business, how we communicate, and how we maintain the state of our health. As stated by Eric Schmidt, the executive chairman of Google: "Technology is always evolving, and companies…can't be afraid to take advantage of change."

As history has shown, no business model is safe from the results of an impactful technology.

Seemingly sensational advances, such as the Supersonic Transport (SST) did not have an impact due to economics while other less glamorous inventions such as the refrigerator, made it possible to safely store foods and reduce illness.

There are offshoots and unintended consequences of technology. Even the humble farmer can make use of advanced technology through the use of satellites to promote "precision farming" and boost crop yields. Orbiting satellites collecting electromagnetic radiation can help match crops with the underlying soil conditions. GPS satellites can also guide a farm tractor to drive itself with great accuracy to ensure the proper application of seed and fertilizer as well as saving fuel.

Just as the invention of the vacuum tube initiated the electronics age, it was soon succeeded by the transistor, which some consider one of the greatest inventions of the 20th century. Transistors, which are the basis for integrated circuits and advanced microprocessors that have themselves, revolutionized society. As microprocessors become more powerful, there are unintended consequences, as you cannot process information without expending energy. The key component of these chips is transistors, which per a trend known as Moore's law, shows a doubling in the number of transistors every two years. Due to the density of the transistors on a chip, the amount of generated heat and power consumed continues to increase. Newer chips based on new materials such as Graphene and nanotubes are just two of a number of technologies being explored in order to reduce the power needs of computers.

The consumerization of IT is associated with the advent of mobile computing devices (e.g., Smartphone's, tablets) with their intuitive functionality, ease-of-use, and low price points. This coupled with data gathering and control devices (e.g., medical monitoring appliances, utility system sensors) and cloud computing, organizations and their leaders are presented with a multitude of challenges. The ubiquitous Internet, The Internet of Things, Cloud computing, the ever increasing volumes of data, and mobile devices can be considered to be 21st century game changers.

The current wave of social, mobile and cloud are all impactful technologies that have exposed users to new approaches for consumers and businesses alike. This has even spawned a buzzword that combines the terms: SoMoClo. These social, mobile and cloud technologies do not exist independently of one another. Enterprise mobile apps tie in to cloud services. The cloud hosts social networks and big data. By adopting a corporate-wide strategy to leverage the trends of SoMoClo, your organization will be better able to drive new innovations and collaboration. The underlying currents of SoMoClo are changing how people engage with each other and within an organization.

We've briefly highlighted several areas that have experienced significant changes due to innovation, technologies, new business models, and market expectations. Disruptive innovation can create great uncertainty for leaders and their organizations. There are no defined best practices or best principles in dealing with either disruptive innovation or the competencies necessary for leading in this environment. A leader requires timely and complete data to help aid in the decision making process. Even in the absence of all of the relevant data, a leader must be comfortable in using whatever information that they have and using their best judgment in reaching a conclusion.

A case in point is Jeff Bezos, CEO of Amazon, who was characterized in a recent Fortune magazine article as "the ultimate disruptor." He has not followed what would be considered as standard policies and Wall Street's pleas for consistent earnings growth. During the 2008 recession, he did not follow conventional wisdom in pulling back on spending as many other companies did; rather invest in building new infrastructure to help build future business. Despite the fact that Bezos is willing to take risks and lose money, investors who have seen an increase in the value of Amazon stock in 2012 have embraced him. *Fortune* has named Bezos its 2012 Businessperson of the Year. (2012 Businessperson of the Year)

While defying conventional wisdom, he has amassed many critics. He summarized the essence of the leadership challenge when he said, "Any time you do something big, that's disruptive, there will be critics… We are willing to be misunderstood for long periods of time". (Jeff Bezos on Innovation, 2011)

How the Internet is changing the World

The Internet Galaxy is a book that was published in 2001 by Manuel Castells, who is widely regarded as the leading analyst of the Information Age. The title is a play on the term "The Gutenberg Galaxy", which was coined by Marshall MacLuhan to describe the influence of printing on the transformation of society. In his book, Castells argues that the Internet, like the printing press, is likely to create a new form of networked society that we are at ground zero of. He believes that we are "entering, full speed, the Internet Galaxy, in the midst of informed bewilderment" and how it is affecting every area of human life--from work, politics, planning, media, and privacy, to our social interaction and life in the home. (Castells, 2001) Microsoft Chairman Bill Gates observed, "The Internet will be to the 21st century what aviation was to the 20th century."

As former president Bill Clinton stated at the announcement of the next generation Internet initiative: "When I took office, only high energy physicists had ever heard of what is called the World Wide Web… Now even my cat has its own page." (Clinton, 1996)

The current Internet as we know it is only the beginning. The next generation Internet will become an omnipresent, all-inclusive network of communicating IOT whereby computing and communications will become ubiquitous, indivisible and invisible. This ubiquitous Internet is one of the main characteristics of the new Internet and a key enabling technology for the evolving global information age.

For the first time in human history, large segments of the world's population can communicate, in real time, with voice, or data, to others. By end 2011, more than one-third of the population (i.e. 2.3 billion people) worldwide was online and that mobile cellular subscriptions reached almost 6 billion by end 2011. (News, 2010)

In 2005 82% of the earth's population lived in range of a mobile network signal. (Union, 2012) As the vast majority of these networks carry data as well as voice, in some form, data transmission ("the Internet") is also ubiquitous. As time progresses, CISCO offers some very interesting statistics in a recent study: Global mobile data traffic grew 70 percent in 2012. Global mobile data traffic reached 885 petabytes per month at the end of 2012, up from 520 petabytes per month at the end of 2011. Last year's mobile data traffic was nearly twelve times the size of the entire global Internet in 2000. Global mobile data traffic in 2012 (885 petabytes per month) was nearly twelve times greater than the total global Internet traffic in 2000 (75 petabytes per month). Mobile video traffic exceeded 50 percent for the first time in 2012. Mobile video traffic was 51 percent of traffic by the end of 2012. (Cisco, 2012)

This communications ability becomes a great equalizer in allowing everyone to "talk to everyone, everywhere and without a costly infrastructure. Recent events such as those related to the Arab spring and the publication of confidential political information on the Internet have demonstrated the power of communication and connectedness and enormously increased political interest in the information society. This communications ability is now moving into corporate America with the blending of video, messaging, data, and voice to improve collaboration. While the underlying technology pieces aren't new, what's new is their combination into an easier-to-use desktop tool that helps facilitate collaborative analysis and problem solving.

The proliferation of smart wireless mobile devices and apps that offer processing capacity is the forerunner for a new era of ubiquitous communications. Users will simultaneously engage different cloud enabled services and capabilities, enabling them to access information and processing capabilities from; anyone, anywhere, and anything.

The Internet of Things

Everything is getting connected as a part of the ubiquitous Internet. The vision of the Internet of Things (IOT) will soon produce a massive volume and variety of data at unprecedented velocity and will create an open, global network that connects people, data and machines. Billions of machines, products and things from the physical and organic world will merge with the digital world allowing near real-time connectivity and analysis. This is sometimes referred to as the Hyper-connectivity of Everything.

Ubiquitous computing is the embedding of computational power into everyday items. This moves intelligence to the edges (e.g., intelligent appliances, smart sensors/objects/structures). Ubiquitous networks is always-on, anyone, anywhere networking that gives network access to anything, allowing everything to become networked.

The Internet of Things is a concept that describes how the Internet will expand as physical items such as consumer devices, sensors, and physical assets are connected to the Internet. The vision and concept have existed for years; however, there has been acceleration in the number and types of things that are being connected and in the technologies for identifying, sensing and communicating that can be linked to traditional IT systems. Beecham Research Limited

(BRL) opens up the broad IT term of Machine to Machine (M2M) that refers to setting up either wireless or wired networks where devices of the same general type and ability can communicate freely.

Bill Ruh, VP and Corporate Officer at General Electric, recently spoke on "Clouds, Big Data and Brilliant Machines" at the Cloud Connect conference in Santa Clara. "We see a transformational change. The change we see is a move from an analog to digital business. We see an architectural shift in how products and services are built... We're not discussing business intelligence. We are discussing deep statistics, machine learning, and modeling to change our understanding of what is happening. This will require a foundational shift in our systems".

Having devices connected via the Internet of Things (IoT) is not enough. They need to be able to connect to scalable resources, such as cloud computing platforms, share diverse, distributed information and intelligently "communicate" to each other.

Some analysts view IoT as the next big technology wave that promises to transform how people interact with the world and make everyone from entrepreneurs to savvy enterprises a to make significant money in the process. Just as the Internet changed the way products and services were marketed and led to new business models and strategies, today's leaders need to consider how the Internet of Things will lead to business transformations that will drive efficiencies and improved how existing services are delivered. Consider the example of sensors being embedded into products that a company purchases that will impact how to manage the supply chain. IoT is likely to bring many new novel business models that will ultimately impact every single industry and our way of life.

What IoT devices can you foresee that your company will be involved with?

Can Leaders Harness The Hyper connectivity of Everything?

Think of the Hyper-connectivity of Everything as the convergence of multiple "Connections": the Connections of Information (World Wide Web and systems), the Connections of People (social networks), the Connections of Things and the Internet of Places. These Connections can produce much value on their own (e.g., social networks), but it is the convergence of the multiple Connections that produces the greatest value, innovation and potential for competitive advantage.

The Hyper-connectivity of Everything will pervade business, government and society, creating new business models and transforming existing ones and successful leaders will be able to harness these new business models and continuously innovate.

As the Hyper-connectivity of Everything develops, everything will have an IP address. The number of Internet-connected entities and the volume of Internet data will increase. Connected objects are driving hyper connected businesses and extended value chains. This interconnectivity of objects, systems, information, people and places is creating many new business opportunities. Risks and issues of security, privacy, Internet network fragmentation and infrastructure congestion may slow or diminish aspects of the Internet of Everything trend and potentially impact the acceleration of innovation.

Are you building new leadership, business, and technology models based on the hyper connectivity of Everything Trend?

Leading Change in a Web 2.1 World

Recent advances in Web 2.0 technology enable new leadership processes and guidelines that can create great value for organizations. In this important new book—the first title in the new Brookings series on Innovations in Leadership—management expert Jackson Nickerson proposes a combination of processes and guidelines utilizing Web 2.0 technology, which he refers to as Web

2.1 that will not only lead and direct change in an organization but actually accelerate it. He calls this set of processes and guidelines "ChangeCasting," and it should be an important part of any organization's leadership toolkit.

Leading Change in a Web 2.1 World provides fresh insights into why people and organizations are so difficult to engage in change. It explains how web-based video communications, when used in accordance with Change Casting principles, can be a keyway to building trust and creating understanding in an organization, thereby unlocking and accelerating organizational change.

Nickerson introduces us to two Fortune 1000 firms facing dire economic and competitive circumstances. Both CEOs attempted extensive organizational change using web-based video communications, but one used Change Casting while the other did not—Nickerson details how Change Casting produced positive financial results for the former. He also discusses how Change Casting principles were used so successfully by the Barack Obama presidential campaign in 2008.

Service Orientation

Software architecture is the computing equivalent to a blueprint of a building in showing all system components and their interactions. Just as a building blueprint has different views (e.g., structural, electrical, plumbing), IT architecture can also be decomposed into multiple views.

These components or Services are constructed so that they can be easily linked with other software components. Service-Oriented Architecture (SOA) is an architectural approach for constructing complex software-intensive systems from a set of universally interconnected and interdependent building blocks, called services. A system based on SOA architecture will provide a loosely integrated suite of services that can be used within multiple separate systems from several business domains. These services can become parts of larger systems that can be connected through standards-based Application Programming Interfaces (APIs). An API is a protocol used as an interface by software components to communicate with each other. A well-developed API can accelerate innovation in a product. Google Maps and the Facebook Like button are actually examples of two extremely popular APIs.

SOA represents a convergence of technology trends and business needs that assist business people understanding rather than as an arcane IT or technical terminology.

According to the Gartner Group, SOA "is a design paradigm and discipline that helps IT meet business demands. Some organizations realize significant benefits using SOA including faster time to market, lower costs, better application consistency and increased agility. SOA reduces redundancy and increases usability, maintainability and value. This produces interoperable, modular systems that are easier to use and maintain. SOA creates simpler and faster systems that increase agility and reduce total cost of ownership (TCO)." (Gartner IT Glossary)

While SOA is about the infrastructure and not about the business process itself, it is a design for the vehicle that helps deliver the business needs to the organization. In SOA, architecture can be separated into two layers. The first layer maintains the direct business relevance as it carries out business functions while the second layer provides the detailed technical basis for the system. SOA can be the lynchpin in helping businesses be more agile and cost effective to ever changing market conditions. It's the services that the businesses are interesting in as opposed to the underlying technologies.

SOA emerged from the concepts of software components and object-oriented programming based on the needs for the economies of scale and agility as computer applications grew in complexity. Other technology drivers were the advent of distributed computing, network-centric computing and the Internet. The business leader must realize that SOA offers protection of existing IT investments without inhibiting the deployment of new capabilities. Through standardized services, the value to the business increases significantly. The cloud now becomes the repository for standardized services.

Several years ago, SOA was considered the IT transformation poster child. Today, the hype curve is around cloud computing. However, looking at the relationships and dependencies between SOA and Cloud Computing as well as their dependences, we find them complementary and synergetic to each other. SOA is the application of business principles into the technology. Cloud is a technical concept, which has had a huge impact on the business. Cloud computing is not just a rendition of SOA; one strongly reinforces the other.

Cloud Computing

The origin of the term cloud computing comes from diagrams of clouds that were drawn to represent the Internet. To facilitate discussion, the cloud provided a layer of abstraction, as it didn't matter where the messages went. This provides a level of generalization that abstracts the complexities of the communications infrastructure, server platforms, applications, and data.

Cloud computing is still an evolving paradigm and probably will be for some time to come. Its definitions use cases, underlying technologies, issues, risks, and benefits will be refined in a spirited debate by the public and private sectors. These definitions, attributes, and characteristics will evolve and change over time. However, it is one of the foundations of the next generation of computing.

The National Institute of Standards and Technology (NIST) formally defines the cloud as, "a model for enabling ubiquitous, convenient, on-demand network access to a shared pool of configurable computing resources (e.g., networks, servers, storage, applications, and services) that can be rapidly provisioned and released with minimal management effort or service provider interaction." (Grance, 2011) Figure 7 depicts a cloud computing visualization from the CIO Research Center. (the nist definition of cloud computing, 2011)

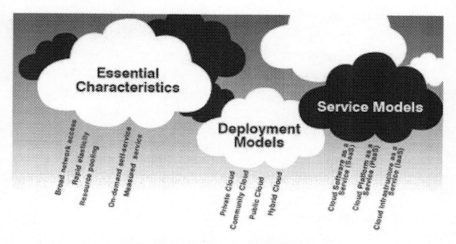

The Cloud Computing Model

Cloud computing has become one of the foundations of the next generation of computing that provides affordable computing power on demand. The cloud offers the ability to scale very rapidly and to operate IT systems more economically that previously possible. Consider Cloud Computing as technology that line-of-business leaders can consume without the limitations of a traditional IT enterprise. It offers improved agility to deploy solutions and choice between cloud service providers and simpler change management of infrastructure.

There are inherent challenges in adopting cloud computing that leaders need to be concerned with that include:

- The loss of control over cloud resources, risk of cloud service provider lock in, reliability, security and data privacy. It's about thinking differently as to how systems are stood up, and getting people out of the mind-set that any kind of new application requires a high up-front cost on new enterprise IT resources. Cloud computing does have the reality that it is based on a complex distributed system. Even though you may not own the hardware or software, you still have to deal with the underlying architecture and its related complexities. Associated with this is the potential of vendor lock-in. Enterprises that are using proprietary vendor technology may incur heavy costs if they to move to another cloud service provider.

- The risk of data and information that now moves into the hands of a third-party provider for storage, processing, or support. This further raises the specter of information security, legal and contractual issues, and data ownership / custodian responsibilities.

- The business model for acquiring computing resources in the cloud, based on usage rather than through purchase or lease of the hardware and software platforms – buying computing rather than computers. This is a shift from capital expenditures (Capex) to operational expenditures (Opex) that are tied to the peaks and troughs of business activities.

- Concerns by current IT staff members (i.e., system administrators) regarding their new roles upon implementation of cloud computing that may augment or replace on-premise data centers.

- The technology impact can be reduced through the use of Cloud Service Brokers – third parties that add value to cloud services on behalf of cloud service customers.

- At the business level, business leaders must set policies for corporate cloud use or will be faced with different organizations purchasing some cloud-based capability through their corporate card with no due diligence.

The economics of cloud computing lets innovative companies create a new generation of products and services that were not previously possible. Many technological business ideas that require prohibitive amounts of computing power or scale could not be implemented either due to cost considerations or technical limitations. Now innovators can use the technical and economic advantages of cloud computing to offer new solutions. This has also given rise to new IT vendors who are capitalizing on opportunities to create new cloud based products and services to fill market niches.

A prime example of cloud computing services is Amazon Web Services (AWS), which offer a wide variety of services (storage, database, computing power, servers, application services, deployment & management) accessible through a set of APIs.

For too long, organizations have been collecting information with the result that many are drowning in a sea of data. The cloud computing paradigm and big data can now help change that.

In the longer term, cloud computing is increasingly appearing to be a transformative and cultural change in the business landscape.

Enterprise Mobility

Enterprise mobility is the trend toward a shift in work habits, with more employees working out of the office and using personal or business-owned mobile devices and cloud services to perform business tasks. Enterprise mobility is poised to fundamentally change the IT landscape. We are now beginning to see a blurring of the boundaries between work and life.

Enterprise mobility refers not only to mobile workers and mobile devices, but also to the mobility of corporate data. The rapidly accelerating pace of the mobility revolution intensifies the pressure on leaders to deliver innovation and transformational leadership to the enterprise. Enterprise Mobility offers the opportunity to innovate their business practices as Smartphone's and tablets offer the chance to improve everything from employee productivity to customer interaction and achieving competitive advantage.

Currently, 54% of adults in the U.S. own smartphones and about 25% own tablets. In roughly three years, the number of tablets alone will overtake the number of PCs. By 2016, about 450 million tablets will be sold annually worldwide. (Luger, 2013)

It's no longer sufficient for organizations to have a simple static informational website, blogs, posts on Facebook or to send tweets to engage with end users. More interactive and creative methods for a sustained two-way dialog need to be applied to maintain and cultivate user interest. The use of smart phones and mobile computing devices, now provide the tools to better facilitate this exchange.

Whether we like it or not, the revolution is here. The consumerization of IT – or BYOD (Bring Your Own Device) – is transforming client computing, as we know it. More and more companies are finding that employees want the freedom to choose the devices they work with. This is putting additional pressure on IT to find ways to safely and securely integrate a variety of new devices into their infrastructures.

Enterprise mobility is a complex topic, but with a focus on user productivity in its ability to help users work smarter and making personal and business activities coexist as seamlessly as possible.

According to a 15th Annual CIO Technology Survey 2012 report from global professional recruitment and executive search firm Harvey Nash USA, one in five CIO's believes that their direct control over technology has diminished since the start of the recession. "There is a strong shift toward a more collaborative and multi-skilled CIO," notes Bob Miano, president and CEO of Harvey Nash USA. In reality, "IT leaders have more influence than ever before, but that influence is increasingly dependent on the CIO's ability to work with others in the organization, particularly the CMO. Only three percent currently believe their organizations innovation potential is being fully realized, and more than two-thirds of CIO's, 69 percent—say they are spending too little time and too few resources on innovation projects. Successful innovations in cloud, mobility and collaboration technology will contribute to greater CIO influence as long as these executives can deliver on expectations," Miano notes. "CIO's require more time and resources to capitalize on this innovation potential. This requires additional support from others in the C-suite." IT leaders who will excel in this new environment will strive for shared goals with partners, both inside and outside the organization. A key to success is improving the return on innovation investment. (Harvey Nash CIO Survey 2013)

Enterprise mobility has become the new mandate for organizations wanting to increase worker productivity and maintain their competitive edge. This enablement of mobile workers to have anywhere, anytime access to enterprise applications and data through their mobile devices is not without its risk. Business users and consumers are downloading applications with little consideration for potential security risks. Not having the proper management solution, technologies and policies in place introduces significant security concerns for the enterprise as well as for individual users. Leaders need to be in front of all of the issues pertaining to Enterprise mobility.

Innovation in Mobile Computing

Mobile apps are some of the most exciting areas of innovation in technology today with amazing growth in this space. Although mobile apps can be quickly developed and distributed, there are a number of complexities to the organization that a leader must contend with. A potential start is for an organization to review and rethink existing business processes to determine how mobile can increase productivity or flexibility. This should be part of an overall digital strategy that considers the impact of mobile on the current enterprise IT architecture. Leveraging a Cloud platform for apps that allows the enterprise to focus on iterating quickly can accelerate mobile application innovation.

Enterprise mobile computing is a significant innovation having impact across all professional disciplines. The future vision for mobile computing is influencing science and technology and mobile applications have been developed to enhance education, access to global scientific references, chemical and biological utilities and medical tool sets.

There are over 750,000 apps in just Apple's App Store, and hundreds of thousands more in Google and Microsoft's stores. But few have had the power and influence to disrupt an entire industry. A small number of these apps have been disruptive industry game changers. Consider a representative small set of innovative uses of mobile computing:

- In Kenya, mobile phones are being used to collect data and report on disease-specific issues from more than 175 health centers serving over 1 million people. This technology has reduced the cost of the country's health information system by 25% and cut the time needed to report the information from four weeks to one week.

- DoctorMole utilizes the camera on a mobile phone to take pictures of pathology and integrate them with Augmented Reality (AR) in order to assess skin moles using the Asymmetry, Border, Color, Diameter and Risk (ABCDE) approach.

- Mobile payment systems are redefining commerce through Smartphone-related payment apps — such as Square and Intuit GoPayment.

- LogMeIn Ignition allows users to access their PC or Mac from their Smartphone or tablet. Business users will be able to quickly access desktop applications from the mobile device such as Office, or their CRM from anywhere in the world.

- Dropbox is the future of storage. Any file you save to your Dropbox is accessible from all your computers, iPhone, iPad, Android device, and even the Dropbox website.

What are some of your favorite business apps?

Big Data

While the data explosion appears to reference the volume of data, that isn't always the case. "Big Data" is a catch phrase that refers to the tools, processes and procedures allowing an organization to create, manipulate, manage, visualize, and store massive and dynamic volumes of both structured and unstructured data that are so large that it's difficult to process using traditional database and software techniques. As with many IT buzzwords, technical terms such as Big Data can have different meanings to different people.

More formally, according to Gartner, Big Data "is high-volume, high-velocity and high-variety information assets that demand cost-effective, innovative forms of information processing for enhanced insight and decision making".

When organizations get to the point where their volume, velocity, variety and veracity of data exceed storage or computing capacity of their legacy IT systems, there are some big challenges that need to be addressed. The large amounts of multi-structured data types have put a strain on conventional transaction-based Data Base Management Systems and data warehouses, which cannot adequately handle the massive volume and velocity requirements of Big Data. Traditional data warehousing typically draw from a limited set of structured data sources and requires an iterative Extract, Transform and Load (ETL) process to prepare the data for business analysis use.

If you think today's Internet generates a lot of data, the Internet of Things raises the stakes significantly. IoT will require massive, scalable, storage and processing capacity, which will invariably reside in the cloud, except for specific localized or security-sensitive cases.

Big Data Innovation

The White House led, Open Government Initiative is making data collected by governments, organizations, and companies, available to everyone, preferably at no cost. A White House directive requires all federal agencies to establish APIs for internal and external developers to use, and make "applicable government information open and machine-readable by default. The content that is created by one organization can be dynamically posted and updated in multiple locations on the Web or mobile application. This dovetails in with the effort to move the U.S. government toward a cloud-computing future. Instead of providing just the raw data, a common set of APIs offer the building block interfaces with the intention of fueling innovative usage of the data.

Data Explosion

The enterprise has gotten comfortable with managing massive amounts of data that drive the business. However, the speed of information creation continues to accelerate. The world contains an unimaginably vast amount of digital information, which is increasing significantly on a daily basis.

The first obvious reasons are the growing number of mobile-phone subscriptions (5.6 billion worldwide) (howmanyarethere.org, 2012) and Internet users (2,459,646,518 internet users worldwide in the February 2012 that represent about 30.2% of the population worldwide), according to Internet World Stats data updated in February 2012.). (how many internet users are there in the world 2012, 2012) This results in an ever-increasing amount of user-generated content that has increased 15-fold over the past few years, according to a Google VP Marissa Mayer made at Xerox PARC. Mayer said during her presentation that this "data explosion is bigger than Moore's law." (McManus, 2010)

As of 2012, about 2.5 Exabytes of data are created each day, and that number is doubling every 40 months or so. More data cross the Internet every second than were stored in the entire Internet just 20 years ago.

Another key aspect is the emerging Internet of Things is the massive amount of new data on the Internet that will result. These new devices and sensors are creating data that was previously unavailable.

Some organizations and businesses are major data collectors from sensors used to gather climate information for the U.S. National Oceanic and Atmospheric Administration (NOAA), posts to social media sites, NASA sensor data from our nearly 100 currently active missions, pharmaceutical drug testing data, digital pictures and streaming videos, geophysical data, and cell phone GPS signals to name a few. It's been estimated that retail giant Wal-Mart handles more than 1 million customer transactions per hour, feeding databases estimated at more than 2.5 petabytes. (Data, Data, Everywhere, 2010)

Cognitive Overload

A recent report from Deloitte focuses on "Cognitive Overload." in which they estimate that the amount of worldwide information doubles every 18 months, and corporate files double every 3.5 years. More than 35 billion e-mails are sent each day. Combine that with Instant Messaging, and Social Media, it becomes clear that the corporate world is experiencing an information overload. (Connecting People to What Matters, 2008)

From a human perspective, cognitive or information overload is a situation whereby an individual has too much information or too many simultaneous tasks and is unable to adequately process this information. Never before in history have we faced the daunting task of making sense of such massive amounts of data. This results in stress and anxiety of decision-making amidst uncertainty, constant change, and financial pressures. Never before in history have individuals been asked to absorb and make sense of so many data points. It's about providing people with the right information at the right time.

Data can be characterized as raw, independent, unorganized values of qualitative or quantitative variables that need to be processed. Information is the result of *data* being processed, organized, structured or presented in a given context so as to make it useful. These terms are often used interchangeably but not truly synonymous. Knowledge is made up of different strands of information. Knowledge discovery and data mining focuses on the process of extracting meaningful patterns from large data sets, using automated computational and statistical tools and techniques.

Based on the sheer volume of data being collected, Big Data analytics is the process and tools to parse data from multiple sources and interactively correlate the data to discover useful information and uncover hidden patterns as actionable information in near real-time. Data that has accumulated over the years opens up options of performing statistics generation, trend analysis and the extrapolation into future expectations.

The unstructured data that has been collected in the past but not analyzed is sometimes referred to as hidden or "dark data". The challenge is to help organizations to uncover all of the hidden information present to make better decisions in support of their business / mission. Big Data technologies tackle both conventional transactional data as well as the multi-structured data that are not addressed by conventional BI tools.

Some of the challenges relating to the processing and storage of Big Data can be leveraged by the capabilities offered by Cloud Computing.

An overabundance of data can result in "paralysis by analysis" in which a decision or action is never taken based on over analyzing the situation, in effect paralyzing the outcome.

Predictive Analytics

The value of big data comes from the knowledge and insights gained from new and emerging types of data and content and what an organization does with it. The collected data now becomes the new raw material of business: an economic input almost on a par with capital and labor. Organizations are in need of solutions that combine both technology and business processes so they can take full advantage of their information to make your business more agile, and to answer questions that were previously considered beyond your reach. Until now, there was no practical way to harvest this opportunity.

Opportunities now exist for leaders to radically learn more about their businesses, and directly translate that knowledge into improved agile decision-making and organizational performance. The big data movement, like analytics before it, seeks to glean intelligence from data and translate that into business advantage. Appropriate analytical processes applied to the data can unlock new sources of business value.

An interesting use of predictive analytics is to understand talent acquisition challenges. Predictive metrics can assist HR in estimating upcoming turnover rates in key jobs and forecast which positions will require recruiting due to growth.

Big data gives us the ability to glean insights out of this deluge of information. According to research by MGI and McKinsey's Business Technology Office, big data analytics "will become a key basis of competition, underpinning new waves of productivity growth, innovation, and consumer surplus" (Big Data: The next frontier for innovation, competition and productivity, 2011)

Traditional business intelligence (and data mining) techniques, in hindsight, do a good job of showing you where you've been. By contrast, predictive analytics uses data patterns to make forward-looking predictions that guide you to where you should go next.

One form of predictive analytics model seeks to find relationships between purchases when certain groups or products are involved. For example, if a customer buys a certain grouping of items, they may be more or less likely to buy another group of items at the same time or at a future date. A fascinating case study in predictive analytics illustrates how Target, America's third biggest retailer, combined data from individual customer purchases with other socio-demographic data obtained from commercial databases to draw strikingly detailed portraits of individual customers. Target's predictive analytics program has been able to deduce whether an individual shopper possesses characteristics that make them particularly susceptible to the specific targeted marketing efforts. In this case, Target's model scored every female Target shopper on pregnancy scale (how likely are they going to be pregnant) to target them for baby/pregnancy related products and also up sell other products, as pregnancy is believed to be one of the events where buying habits can be influenced more readily. (Duhigg, 2012)

The knowledge gained from the analysis of big data can be the basis for making decisions or taking actions that are important to the company and is defined by its use and its relevance to work.

The study further states that within the next few years, millions of big data-related IT jobs will be created worldwide. However, there is a major shortage of the "analytical and managerial talent necessary to make the most of big data." The United States alone faces a shortage of more than 140,000 workers with big data skills as well as up to 1.5 million managers and analysts needed to analyze and make decisions based on big data findings.

According to the MIT Center for Digital Business, companies that adopt data-driven practices, and use big data to guide decision-making, "will have output and productivity that is 5 to 6 percent higher than what would be expected given their other investments and information technology uses". (MIT Computer Science and Artificial Intelligence Lab, 2013)

In an increasingly competitive global marketplace, innovative leaders have to do everything they can to stay ahead of their competition by harnessing the data and information around them.

Social Media

One of the key sources of vast quantities of data that are being fed into the cloud every day is social media. The explosion in the use of Google, Facebook, Twitter, YouTube and other social networking web sites has resulted in the generation of some 2.5 quintillion bytes each day. Organizations are beginning to understand the vast intelligence that can be derived by looking at millions of conversations taking place, mostly out in the open, between those engaging in social media.

Use of web-based and mobile technologies, social media has become the new communication mechanism for interactive dialog amongst individuals. Going far beyond other conventional media types that share information, such as newspapers, radio or television, social networking tools like Twitter, Facebook, and Blogs have facilitated creation and exchange of ideas so quickly and widely.

Consider the following two examples:

- The aftermath of the 2010 Haitian earthquake resulted in a loss of, many communications capabilities. To facilitate the sharing of information and make up for the lack of information, social media came in very handy to report the news about the affected area on what happened and what help was needed. Tweets from citizenry, aid workers provided a view of the ongoing events and rescue efforts. News organizations such as the BBC covered the event by combining tweets and live Blogs together with the information from other news organizations to develop a grasp of the situation

- The social media's growing influence throughout the world was shown during the 2011 Middle East "Arab Spring" protests. The protesters, media, and journalists made extensive use of social networking sites, tweeting and texting on the protests, with the messages read and commented on by people world-wide. Social media was instrumental in helping the movement achieve critical mass.

The application of natural language processing and analytical processing techniques are now being used to gain a better understanding of attitudes, trends and sentiments found within social media. Companies such as Best Buy are using social media tools to mine comments on the Web to see what consumers really think of their products and services. Extracting insight from text and analyzing sentiment in online conversations around specific topics can be a leading indicator in predicting outcomes. While positive or negative sentiment may be difficult to discern and provide sometimes-questionable accuracy in its resultant analysis, it does help wade through the abundance of both relevant and irrelevant information generated in social media. However, it is non-trivial, such to make analytic sense of content types such as pictured embedded within tweets, high definition video, or sensing the connections between the thousands of natural language messages.

While privacy, legal, and regulatory issues exist in dealing with social media; it's unlikely to delay the growing adoption of such capabilities, given their potential value. Social media is not really about technology. It's about a cultural shift that is enabled by the evolution of technology.

But human-generated social-media data is essentially unstructured and not conforming to any pre-defined data model, which makes it so difficult to manage and analyze. This is now being augmented with similarly unstructured business content, which takes many forms (i.e., emails, instant messages, reports, presentations, PDF documents, spreadsheets). Unstructured content is fundamentally different from structured data and must be treated in an entirely different way. Unstructured data represents that conversation and context.

Aside from social media use within society as a whole, there is now the rise of social media as a business application and the blurring between work and home as driven by the emergence of new mobile devices. Externally, public social media platforms like Facebook and Twitter can help an organization stay close to their customers. Internally, a variety of enterprise social tools like Yammer can improve communication and collaboration between employees.

What social media tools does your company utilize?

Chapter Seven
Impact of Advanced Sensors and Ubiquitous Computing

*Computing will become as ubiquitous
as dust, but much more impactful.*
—Melvin Greer

Advanced sensors and ubiquitous computing will make data readily available and have a significant impact on the kinds, ways and speed with which we are able to make decisions and enable other new technologies.

There are different names for this growing phenomenon of aware and interconnected objects. "The Internet of Things" is the most popular one, but other names include "machine-to-machine (M2M) technology" and "ubiquitous computing." I like this last one as it gets at the heart of this sea change.

Sure, we can connect a bunch of things to the Internet. But the hubbub is not about connecting things to the Internet; it's about putting computers everywhere.

Think about it. We might feel like we're surrounded by computers all right: each one of us probably carries three or four on our person at a time, if we've got a laptop bag with an e-reader or tablet and a mobile phone. And most of us own plenty of appliances that contain computers, and drive cars that contain computers. We're aware that computers now run things like traffic lights and elevators.

But imagine if there was a computer in literally every object in your house, in your office, in your neighborhood. Imagine computers were in the wind. Imagine if they were literally ubiquitous. That would really be something.

I think about sensors the same way I think about mobile phones. Those very first mobile phones—the ones with the shoulder straps and the battery pack—were kind of a game-changer, but not really. They let you use a phone in your car, but they were heavy, and you were still tethered, and they had this giant battery that you had to lug around. They were cool as a concept, but they didn't change daily life much.

Smartphone's are the game-changer as they are the Internet, in your pocket. They're amazing! But that didn't happen overnight; it took a lot of iterations to get there. The technology had to evolve, and at some point it made a kind of phase shift.

Similarly, the types of DIY sensors that organizations and journalists are starting to build are not the game-changer. They're the pre-cursor, the ancestor, to what will change our lives. And smart dust, or the beginnings of it, will be a step along the way. I don't know what the real game-changer will look like. It will probably be physically small, yes. But will it be something like smart dust?

My bet is that it will do things we can't even dream about yet—in the same way that the Victorians might have imagined bringing the town center to residents, but they never dreamed of Amazon.

The important thing, though, is that sometimes you can predict the "what" even if you don't yet know the "how." So here are a few things I believe to be true about the way sensors will affect us in the far future.

We will measure, not calculate.

First, we will measure, not calculate. That seems boring on first blush. But think about the kinds of information we approximate, guess at, or determine by polling and sampling, and then making a calculation. In the far future of sensors, we won't have to calculate; we'll measure.

You've probably heard the quote, "You can't manage what you can't measure." It is usually attributed to W. Edwards Deming, a statistician and professor, although he never actually said that. What he did say is, "The most important figures that one needs for management are unknown or unknowable... but successful management must nevertheless take account of them."

There are still some things that sensors won't help us measure, like human motivations. But for the most part, they will bring into the realm of the knowable all kinds of things that we couldn't know before. This will help us better manage our world and ourselves. Deming wasn't saying that you can't manage what you can't measure; he was saying that even though you can't measure it, you still have to find a way to manage it. Sensors are going to make that task far, far easier.

When a bridge on the Skagit River in Washington State collapsed recently, Mike Wheatley wrote a great piece for Silicon Angle on smart bridges and infrastructure sensors. People, engineers monitor most of our nation's aging freeways and bridges. And there just aren't enough of them to go around.

Some of the world's newer bridges are being built with sensors inside, to measure things like vibration. But they are still large, and pretty widely dispersed; when they detect a problem, it still takes a human to come and pinpoint the exact danger or stress point. Imagine how much easier smart dust (or something like it) could make infrastructure monitoring, and how many lives might be saved.

And let me tell you: bridges are one thing, but people are another—another thing we're going to be able to measure. This is going to further the field that is becoming known as precision medicine. Right now, we have drugs that we say work, for example, 80% of the time, when the reality is that they work 100% of the time for 80% of the people. Sensors and other technologies will allow us to divide ourselves into smaller and smaller demographic groups, eventually reaching a demographic of one, so that we know exactly which interventions work for which people.

We will expect to know everything.

I think we will eventually come to the point where nearly everything is known. But I realize how vast the unknown still is when compared to the known, at this point, so let's go with, "we'll increase what we know by an order of magnitude or two."

But who will know it? Right now, the data from the sensors we already have is largely locked away in proprietary silos. Cell phone providers have it. Municipal governments have it. Nike, or Fitbit, or the company that made your pacemaker has it.

I think that things are this way right now mostly because we still default to expecting not to know things—even with the Internet already in our pockets. But that will change. And when it does, the movements already afoot to liberate information from these silos will only intensify. We will expect to be able to know.

When we don't or can't know, things will go awry. One of my colleagues in the Data Sensing Lab, Alasdair Allan, gave a talk at Strata in London last fall, where he said:

> "In the near future, the absence of data about you—about your location—is going to be increasingly unusual. ... 'Innocent until proven guilty' is a core tenant in our legal system, but it came from an age that was data poor. We no longer live in that age."

How will the ubiquity of sensor data change our legal system? Will we go from reasonable doubt to reasonable suspicion?

Of course, there will always be limits to what sensor data can tell us. Alex Howard, wrote: "Data, on its own, locked up or muddled with errors, does little good. Cleaned up, structured, analyzed and layered into stories, data can enhance our understanding of the most basic questions about our world, helping journalists to explain who, what, where, how and why changes are happening."

The who, what, and where are things that sensors are going to tell us a lot about, but the how and why are things we're still going to have to determine for ourselves. Journalists are going to remain a key part of doing that.

We will expect to know everything NOW.

The ability to delay gratification is a skill worth having. But there are times when delay can do us great harm—most notably, when we're trying to learn. Feedback loops are incredibly important when it comes to learning and behavior change. Think of putting your hand on a hot stove: the instant feedback helps you learn not to do it twice in a row. The farther you separate the action from the effect (or the consequence of that action), the harder it is for humans and animals to learn.

Part of the reason that cigarettes are so dangerous is that their feedback loop is sometimes 60 years long. Fatty and sugary foods have a shorter feedback loop, but still not short enough for most people. And the positive actions we can take to combat these harmful things also have long feedback loops. With sensor networks, not only will we know almost everything; we'll be able to know almost right away.

This is the part where I come to the defense of the Quantified Self (QS) movement: the community of people who are interested in (or in many cases, obsessed with) measuring and quantifying their own habits, such as sleeping, eating, and exercising.

Some people have pooh-poohed this movement as an example of technology enabling the ultimate form of narcissism, and would argue that the Internet of Things is in this category as well. But the brilliance of QS is that it has found a way, using sensors, to begin shortening the feedback loop on our most basic behaviors, allowing us to learn, and to change our habits.

Quantified Self is great. But I'm really excited about the prospect of a Quantified Planet movement; Hewlett-Packard is already working on a so-called Central Nervous System for the Earth (CeNSE). Smart dust (or whatever its actual future) is going to make this possible. It's going to let us learn the hard lessons, and change our behaviors in the most critical ways. (And at a time when climate change looms larger than ever, we have a lot of learning to do.)

But here's the kicker: we're not the only ones who learn. Computers learn, too, and the more data we can collect, the better we can teach them (or in many cases, they can teach themselves). All jokes about the Terminator aside, smart machines are going to make our lives better in amazing ways. We will be connected to our environments, and they to us.

The present has to change.

If you listen to some of the television reports about smart dust, they're amusing. "Smart dust on the tracks will monitor your commuter train so you can know if it's running late," says one. This is delightfully short-sited, in that it assumes that we will continue to wait for trains as we always have. The beauty of smart dust (and other sensors) is that it can turn all that on its head. Perhaps it will tell the train system when there is a gathering quorum of passengers on the platform, and a train will be sped along to accommodate them.

This is a small example. But sensors won't just tell us more about the way we're living; they're going to change the way we live.

These open questions remain: What will the far future actually look like? How will sensors help us measure things so that we can better manage them? What stories will we tell about the "how" and "why" of what we measure? I can't tell you yet, but I already know that the future of sensor journalism is one to watch.

Chapter Eight
Harnessing Disruptive Forces

Innovation accelerates and compounds.
Each point in front of you is bigger
than anything that ever happened
                                        —Marc Andreessen

Innovation is key to long-term survival of an organization. It means radically re-evaluating areas of your business that include business strategies, business processes, operations and organizational structures.

There are different approaches to harnessing innovation that include:

- Listen. When you're sitting in a meeting or wandering the hallways, keep your ears open for issues or problems that keep coming up. That will give you ideas for business problems in need of solutions.

- Lead. "You do not lead by hitting people over the head - that's assault, not leadership." --Dwight D. Eisenhower

- Personal Trust. "Outstanding leaders go out of the way to boost the self-esteem of their personnel. If people believe in themselves, it's amazing what they can accomplish." --Sam Walton

- Stay abreast of industry trends. Read trade journals to find out what's going on with your competitors. Understand at a granular level what's driving your company's sales. For example, if you work in the retail industry, you should know what's selling, what's not selling.

- Leverage technology or information differently. You know what you've implemented and you know it better than anyone else in the company, so think of other ways that technology or information can be applied or harnessed.

- Participate in internal and external peer idea exchanges as well as your team for ideas. "Good leaders make people feel that they're at the very heart of things, not at the periphery. Everyone feels that he or she makes a difference to the success of the organization. When that happens people feel centered and that gives their work meaning." --Warren G. Bennis

- Leverage your knowledge from prior companies and industries you've worked in.

- Strategic Alignment. Align innovation and its importance to business strategies.

- Maintain a journal - Many creative individuals keep a journal to write down ideas and thoughts. One of the most noted journals is the Codex Leicester, one of the notebooks left by Leonardo Da Vinci. Bill Gates purchased this famous notebook for $30.8 Million dollars in 1994.

Today's innovation process requires the leveraging of employees, consumers, key stakeholders, and any associated third parties in order to garner any insights that they may hold. An open environment is required to actively engage these participants in the innovation process. This has spawned a new term called Innovation management, which is defined as the collection and collaboration of ideas and the processes involved in advancing development.

Even those companies that seemingly do the right thing such as listening and interacting with customers, keeping watch over their competitors, following the marketplace, and investing in R&D, Clayton Christensen, author of The Innovator's Dilemma, believes that companies can still falter. The author argues that, while existing thriving companies can be successful with sustaining technologies, these same companies often falter with the advent of disruptive technologies. Christensen has categorized technological innovation as either sustaining or disruptive. Sustaining innovations are those that sustain an organization's existing customer base through some added value to an existing product or service (e.g., improved performance, capacity, reliability, lower cost, etc.). Disruptive innovations produce products that differ from the perspective of a firm's existing customer base

They either often do not want to put their resources into developing the new technology, because their existing customer do not want it or they attempt to fit the new technology into the existing market instead of looking to create new markets for the new product which generally doesn't work. (Christensen, 2011)

Instilling Innovation in Leadership

As we start a new year during a slow recovery, innovation will be at a premium as organizations strive to uncover new opportunities for growth. Yet many leaders have trouble thinking about (let alone driving) innovation when they're focused on managing through the still-challenging present.

Five years ago, General Electric (GE) launched a leadership development program called "Leadership, Innovation and Growth" (LIG) to stimulate growth and innovation from within the organization. The program created new ways to think and talk about innovation simply and practically, so it would grow into part of how leaders operated their business. Leadership teams from across GE's top 60 businesses have since participated in the program, and have learned how to translate innovative ideas and opportunities into initiatives with real results.

As GE prepares to launch the next iteration of LIG (focused on global growth), they have spent some time reflecting on what's worked and what needs improvement. The factors most responsible for LIG's success have value and relevance far beyond GE, especially in a slow-growth world. Organizations can teach innovation to their leaders and teams—so these employees can make what they learn in the classroom part of how they operate day to day. Here's the execution road map.

- Keep development teams intact. This is one of the simplest yet most differentiating aspects of teaching innovation. Leadership development programs often fall short of driving real change because managers don't go through the learning process together. Bringing together an entire team for a few days helps build consensus more quickly and fosters a greater commitment to applying new strategies across the operation.

- Secure leadership support. GE views ongoing learning as part of the job, and it reinforces the message from the top down, with current Chief Executive Officer Jeffrey Immelt participating in LIG and other development programs. Without the company's full commitment to providing its leadership bench the necessary time, resources, and ideas, workers will see management programs as a waste of time.

- Leverage actionable frameworks. GE applies a "three-box" framework to strategic planning that helps leaders balance managing through the present, which is largely about driving efficiencies, and creating the future, which is about innovation. Translating a concept like innovation into a workable framework enables leaders and their teams to apply new strategies with consistency and rigor across the organization.

- Create a common language. Similar to making actionable frameworks for innovation, constructing a common vocabulary team members can easily understand and adopt greatly improves chances that they will use what they learn.

- Conduct extensive follow-up. This might seem obvious, but all too often development programs end once people leave the classroom. You can increase the impact of training by retaining various touch points to see how participants integrate innovation strategies into everyday operations. Follow-up can take various forms, whether through workshops or ongoing consulting and guidance, but they should all focus on equipping leaders with tools and a framework they can easily apply.

- Share best practices. As successes emerge, leaders should encourage teams to share them—both to maintain the momentum of what's been learned and drive further adoption across the organization.

Company leaders have two jobs to do. The first is to make money, but the other—and perhaps more challenging—is to invest in the future. Leadership training programs should encourage leaders to think far beyond driving today's efficiencies. Through LIG, GE leadership teams come together on a recurring basis for this time to think in order to ensure learning happens continuously and that it's part of the operating cycle. Innovation, especially in a slow-growth world, won't happen solely through R&D investment in technology; R&D also means investing in people, to equip them to position their business for the future.

Innovation Found in Female Leadership Traits

It may be time for you to tap into your "female" side in order to succeed in today's business environment, according to the book, Social Nation: How to Harness the Power of Social Media to Attract Customers, Motivate Employees, and Grow Your Business (Wiley/Available now). Author Barry Libert contends that the profound cultural shift that's taking place as social networks grow in popularity will raise the value of executives whose management style includes traits that have been traditionally considered "female."

Primary Traits listed include;

- Listening
- Knowing what you are not
- Sharing Rewards
- Understanding that Business is Personal

Libert's premise depends, of course, upon your face-value acceptance of broad gender generalizations. Fair warning: Your individual life experiences may vary. Nonetheless, he claims that all of his conclusions are backed by scientific research. "There have been countless studies on gender differences," Libert says. "And no matter how you interpret them, they conclude that women are collaborative, communicative and community-centered." So, before you cry foul, stop and consider these eight "female traits" from Social Nation that you can turn into leadership action items in your enterprise, regardless of your actual gender.

Do leadership traits traditionally considered female lead to an increase in innovation?

Harnessing Innovation Requires Embracing a Risk Mentality

Who are the leaders that harness innovation? It's not the ones that sit back and takes no chances. A lot of us have tendencies that incline us to avoid risk. It's much easier to take the safe path. And, honestly, there's nothing wrong with being safe. But just as being safe reduces your risk of failure, it also reduces your risk of success. Innovation requires the ability to embrace risks where there is potential for payoff. Who are the leaders that drive innovation by embracing risk? They include people like:

Business owners cannot build innovative businesses by being risk averse. They take financial and personal risks.

Innovative sales people have to go out every day and risk rejection in order to sell their products. You cannot sit at home (or at your desk) and expect customers to call. If you are easily upset at being told no, you wouldn't be innovative in this area.

Corporate leaders didn't get there by keeping their head down and doing precisely what their bosses asked of them. They looked for new opportunities. They suggested new paths for the business. They made decisions that perhaps the rest of us wouldn't make, because others might think they are stupid. They didn't go home at night and complain that they weren't being promoted. They asked for promotions, spoke up in meetings, and put themselves in the path of rejection every day.

Innovators didn't achieve genius status just by drawing one picture, designing one ad campaign or auditioning for one play. They succeed because they recognize that they have something to offer and they do not give up. They show their portfolios. They play their violins for audition after audition. They seek out feedback, teachers and mentors to show them where their mistakes are and what they can do better.

How do you embrace risk? Have you achieved innovation by understand risk potential?

Can You Spot an Innovative Opportunity?

Innovation happens when a team comes up with something brand new and brings it to market with astonishing success. But innovation does not always have to be about launching The Next Big Thing. CIO's, for example, constantly depend upon innovation to keep their organizations ahead of competitors. This quiz tests your knowledge of the kinds of innovations that enabled companies across a wide range of industries to achieve success. Can you spot the innovative concept with the company that put this innovation to good use? Questions and answers are based on the case studies featured in the book "Breaking Away: How Great Leaders Create

Innovation That Drives Sustainable Growth – And Why Others Fail". (Jane Stevenson, 2011)

Q: When customers said they didn't want to post their photographs on social network sites, which cosmetic company came up with a digital, customized "perfect look" tool that women could have e-mailed directly to them?

> A: Estee Lauder, as part of its "Your Beauty, Your Style, and Your Profile" campaign. Key Takeaway: Listen and learn from your customers' comments on Web sites and in social media.

Q: Which toy company used the power of narrative to turn a $30 million product into a $500 million-plus brand?

> A: Hasbro, which sparked a sales surge and movie franchise by creating intriguing plot lines to revive Transformers. Key Takeaway: Use good storytelling to sell your vision.

Q: Which business had achieved innovation by answering this question: "If file-sharing works for addresses, documents, music and movies, why can't it transfer voice data?"

> A: Skype, which found no reason not to make it happen. Key takeaway: Innovation often stems from asking: "Why not?"

Q: Which food giant broke off a brand's highly associated alignment with one particular product to embrace a more diversified approach?

> A: Kraft, which greatly expanded its customer base by promoting Philadelphia Cream Cheese as a food for desserts, late-night snacks, tailgating, etc. Key takeaway: Think about broader applications for existing resources.

Can you think of other examples that demonstrate the critical ability to spot an innovative opportunity?

Crowd Sourcing Innovation

Can innovative idea generation succeed when working with collaborators? Is it better to have lots of innovative ideas to choose from, or a few of higher quality? The answer will help you decide whether you approach hundreds of idea-generators using a technique known as crowd sourcing or bring together a few brilliant minds. Innovation requires both, and here's when to use what.

Quantity and quality serve different purposes. Quantity gives a better chance to receive innovative ideas. But high-quality collaboration is useful when trying to assess all these opportunities. Highly skillful collaborators can help you to better interpret this wealth of insights, to recognize the value of ideas that is not often visible at first, especially when it comes to radical change, and to identify a novel strategic direction.

In short, if quantity is good for creating ideas, quality is good for setting a vision. That's a useful standard to explore the next time you are tasked to develop an innovative new capability or product. Cast a wide net for ideas from customers, your marketing team, your R&D team, and even competitors. With that list in hand, convene a trusted team of collaborators who can envision the best strategic direction these ideas present for growth.

Have you used crowd sourcing to accelerate your innovation planning? What pros and cons have you experienced?

Whitespace Opportunities

In Information Technology, whitespace is any character or series of characters that represents horizontal or vertical space in typography. In communications, white space pertains to the sections of unoccupied and unlicensed spectrum left between communications bands already in use. However, in a business context, whitespace refers to markets or businesses that are outside their primary core that contain potential opportunities.

This is in contrast to Blackspace that encompasses all the business opportunities that a company has formally targeted and organized itself to capture.

Whitespace opportunities in innovation usually pertain to areas where products or services don't currently exist or underserved markets outside of their core. Consumer behaviors are constantly changing and new technologies are always emerging. In our highly competitive global marketplace, any company that wants to remain relevant must intelligently respond to shifting conditions and keep an eye on potential whitespace activities

Several best-selling and renowned business books have analyzed current successful companies with the premise that if you make some generalizations about them, you too can succeed.

In their book, Built to Last, by James Collins and Jerry Porras (James Collins, 1990) , the authors began with the premise that visionary companies start with a great idea and are driven by charismatic leaders. Much to the surprise of the authors, these were two of the shattered myths found to generally be not true. As a part of their own six-year comprehensive, well-documented research study, which was the basis for the book, they found that all visionary companies had a number of connecting key themes for what made them "built to last": "Premier institution in its industry, widely admired by knowledgeable business people, made an indelible imprint on the world in which we live, had multiple generations of chief executives, been through multiple product life cycles, and founded before 1950." Few of these companies started with a great idea.

> "I skate where the puck is going to be, not where it has been." —Wayne Gretzky, hockey player

The book, Seizing the White Space: Business Model Innovation for Growth and Renewal by Mark Johnson believes that promising white space areas include transforming existing markets and creating new markets, in order to confront industry-wide upheaval. Johnson also counts retail discounters like Target, Wal-Mart, and Amazon as white space innovators - they now hold 76% of the retail industry's capitalization. In each of these cases, new business models were created to fill gaps in the market. By making products and services available to individuals for whom existing offerings are potentially too expensive, complicated, or inaccessible

Johnson claims that 30% of the innovations he's studied involved the Internet. Taking advantage of white space opportunities requires a compelling customer value proposition, a winning profit formula, and key resources and processes. A significant barrier usually requires overcoming internal resistance to change. According to Johnson, "White space" is where the opportunity is a poor fit with the existing organization and the customers are either new to the organization or "existing customers served in fundamentally different ways." (Johnson, 2010)

A case cited by Johnson is Tata Motors, when in 2003, Ratan Tata, president of Indian carmaker Tata Motors, saw the danger in entire families riding atop a single motor scooter to travel the crowded streets of New Delhi. The white space that he envisioned was a "people's car" as a safer alternative that would appeal to Indian families who previously could only afford to travel by scooter. The Tata Nano, as the world's least expensive care, was to sell for about US $2000, in order to deliver its customer value proposition to scooter families. For a variety of reasons, to date, the car sales have been disappointing.

There is a strong tendency for companies to discard opportunities that do not belong to the current core. The key to success is the ability to adopt new models outside of the organization's core to seize new opportunities.

Innovation powered by Entrepreneurship

Entrepreneurial thinkers power innovation. The number of entrepreneurship courses nationally has grown from 250 in 1985 to more than 5,000. This is now the hottest degree for the ambitious with dreams of becoming billionaires before age 29. At the Extreme Entrepreneurship Tour, a series of conferences for aspiring young entrepreneurs, hundreds of high school and college kids were feverishly taking notes. The tour, which is only five years old, will attract an estimated 20,000 students this year. All this activity is in response to a critical innovation gap. What is the innovation gap and how can the risks associated with it be mitigated?

Reviewing sources of innovation in 25 consumer product categories over 50 years reveals a growing innovation gap. From the 1960s to the 1980s, 64 percent of all major new innovations came from large corporations (more than $1 billion in revenue). During the past two decades, only 16 percent of innovations came from large companies, while 84 percent of them came from startups or small companies.

In corporations, disruptive innovation has always been somewhat serendipitous. Senior managers or chief executive officers rarely plan great corporate innovations. To have any chance of finding that next "New Thing," you need entrepreneurial-minded people in the lower- to middle-management ranks pushing the boundaries and challenging the organization. Only now those people are opting out of the corporate experience altogether and getting venture capital funding to compete with the large firms they shun. The resources available to budding entrepreneurs are growing each day. Twenty years ago, there were few role models and fewer resources. Today there is a growing ecosystem of support.

The true benefit of entrepreneurs is that they think in terms of business models and can provide strategic and business planning solutions in addition to clever ideas. Organizations are in critical need of people who have an innovative entrepreneurial spirit and who can contribute a risk taking and failure forward culture.

Are you developing an innovative entrepreneurial spirit inside a large corporation? What success are you having in closing the innovation gap?

Experimentation and Prototyping

Today, regardless of their size, every business organization needs a viable business model. A business model describes the rationale of how an organization creates, delivers, and captures value (economic, social, cultural, or other forms of value). A business model articulates how a business creates and delivers value to customers.

> The entrepreneur always searches for change, responds to it, and exploits it as an opportunity. — Peter F. Drucker

In today's global economy, a company can create a competitive advantage by doing something differently e adopting a new business model.

Advances in cloud computing offer a greater tolerance for innovation and experimentation from businesses. Key drivers have been the emergence of the ubiquitous Internet, cloud computing, enterprise communications, and big data. These technologies are offering increasingly lower cost and different approaches for businesses to be more efficient.

New business models are being created that depend completely on the emergent or existing technology. Through the use of such technology to create models, businesses have a better scope to reach large audiences within minimal costs. With fewer technical and economic barriers, cloud computing will enable prototyping and market validation of new approaches across the business domain

(IT, marketing, sales, service) much faster and less expensively that before.

Reinventing a business model requires creative leadership, focused experimentation and industry innovation to pursue growth in today's global markets. Conventional approaches have been enhancing existing product offerings through R&D, or growth through acquisition or moving into new or adjacent markets. A new approach labeled 'business model experimentation' has emerged that explores explore alternative value creation and business model approaches through "thought experiments." The goal is to engage small focused teams to perform these experiments both rapidly and inexpensively to pursue any given idea prior going into the marketplace.

Business model experimentation as a potent source of competitive advantage by innovating across and defining a winning Business Model might be the game changer your organization needs. Several key examples of revolutionary business models include McDonalds, fast food; Wal-Mart, hypermarkets; FedEx, time-effective package delivery; Amazon.com, brick and mortar-less dot-com shopping; Dell Computer; Starbucks, high-end coffee shops; Netflix, fast movie delivery.

Those organization that are too slow to adopt the benefits while managing experimentation and prototyping are likely going to face serious and growing economic and business disadvantage. It takes several iterations to find a business model that works on the ground and has the potential to scale.

When employees become comfortable in their work environment, their natural inclination is to resist changing that comfort level. They become resistant to any new ideas and prefer the status quo. Any efforts, such as experimentation and prototyping can be met with resistance. This is where effective leadership comes in to play to convince that change is good for the organization and that change will be good for them as well.

A question that a successful business may be concerned with is why should they change, especially if everything is working well. Most assuredly, the competition is evolving and if you don't move with the times then the competition will literally wipe you out. Organizations face rapid change like never before. Change means different things to different people and can impact them in different ways. As President Woodrow Wilson once stated, "If you want to make enemies, try to change something." Change can involve entire organizations or just segments of the business; be major or minor in scope; or be of different time durations.

Effective leaders need to map out the future by making organizational changes, strategic decisions about the business that will ensure an exciting future. Leaders have a challenge in convincing the employees that change is good for them and the company.

> "Willingness to change is a strength, even if it means plunging part of the company into total confusion for a while". —Jack Welch

Some of the reasons people react differently to change and may resist change are:

- Fear of the future
- Fear of failure
- Reduced pay or benefits
- Loss of power or position
- Lack of trust in their leadership

As Peter Senge, director of the MIT Sloan School of Management has stated, "People don't resist change. They resist being changed!"

Planning for change is as important as deciding and initiating the change. At the end of the day, all organizations want to move to a better state of affairs, as opposed to a worse state of affairs. Every leader needs to look out over the organization and assess how they can best achieve the change.

The idea is to move as quickly as possible from concept to prototype to test, and then iterate until you land on a business model configuration that works and is ready to scale. Along the way there will be many failures.

It is not the strongest of the species that survive, nor the most intelligent, but the one most responsive to change. – Charles Darwin

Whether as a part of the normal business cycle or as a part of experimenting and prototyping new business models, there are certain outcomes.

"Failure" is one word that always touches on a very sensitive nerve. As a society, failure is treated negatively and upon experiencing it, we want to quickly recover from it and forget that it ever happened.

Most organizations don't create an environment where failure is recognized for its value. How many times have you heard, "We've already tried that and it was a total loss." ? NASA learned much from the ill-fated Apollo 13 moon mission, which had gripped the world in April 1970. The mission itself was characterized by Jim Lovell as "a 'successful failure' because it was a failure in its initial mission -- nothing had really been accomplished," but as "a great success in the ability of people to take an almost certain catastrophe and turn it into a successful recovery."

While we realize that failures can be instructive, failure is usually dismissed and seen as a loss prior to moving on to other potential opportunities. Failures can provide us with our most valuable learning experiences if we choose to learn from them instead of just recovering from them. Failure is an extreme opportunity to learn from and a good leader should not pass it by without garnering as much information out of it as possible.

Failures or negative outcomes are a part of life and are as important to learn from as our successes. Both successes and failures can be instructive. Bogus conclusions and false predictions will occur if we ignore looking at one without the other.

The high-stakes strategy by biopharma companies to develop new drugs involves prolonged and costly clinical trials. According to a U.S. Food and Drug Administration (FDA), report, it presently takes 15 years for drug development and 95% of drug candidate fail along the way.

(Critical Path Initiative, 2009) And most of those that do make it to market; there are those that fail to generate a positive return on investment. In the context of clinical trials, "negative" is often a misnomer. Clinical studies that yield unexpected or undesirable results are infrequently negative in the sense of revealing actual harm to patients from the drug being tested. A "negative" study simply fails to show that it's effective for certain indications, or uses. The end result is that is needed to know about developing a new drug is buried in our past failures.

Two notable quotes come to mind:

> "Would you like me to give you a formula for success? It's quite simple; double your rate of failure. You are thinking of failure as the enemy of success. But it isn't at all. You can be discouraged by failure or you can learn from it. So go ahead and make mistakes. Make all you can. Because remember that's where you will find success." —Thomas J. Watson

> "There are no secrets to success. It is the result of preparation, hard work, and learning from failure." —General Colin Powell

Failures improve your ability in judgment and decision-making. Innovative companies would be less innovative if people weren't comfortable with taking risks for fear of severe penalties.

Here is a response to a question on innovation that Jeff Bezos gave at Amazon.com's 2011 shareholder meeting: "If you invent frequently and are willing to fail, then you never get to the point where you really need to bet the whole company. AWS (Amazon Web Services) also started about six or seven years ago. We are planting more seeds right now, and it is too early to talk about them, but we are going to continue to plant seeds. And I can guarantee you that everything we do will not work. And, I am never concerned about that. We are stubborn on vision; we are flexible on details... We don't give up on things easily. Our third-party seller business is an example of that. It took us three tried to get the third party seller business to work. We didn't give up. But if you get to a point where you look at it and you say look, we are continuing to invest a lot of money in this, and it's not working and we have a bunch of other good businesses, and this is a hypothetical scenario, and we are going to give up on this. On the day you decide to give up on it, what happens? Your operating margins go up because you stopped investing in something that wasn't working. Is that really such a bad day?

So my mind never lets me get in a place where I think we can't afford to take these bets, because the bad case never seems that bad to me. And, I think to have that point of view, requires a corporate culture that does a few things. I don't think every company can do that, can take that point of view. A big piece of the story we tell ourselves about who we are, is that we are willing to invent....

I believe that if you don't have that set of things in your corporate culture, then you can't do large-scale invention. You can do incremental invention, which is critically important for any company. But it is very difficult – if you are not willing to be misunderstood. People will misunderstand you". ". (Jeff Bezos on Innovation, 2011)

Chapter Nine

Case Studies of Leaders
that are Innovating

*A Good innovation leader creates an
environment where…sacred traditions
can be challenged and addressed*
—Elaine Dundon

Throughout this book we have described the need for a new
leadership and innovation model and how we can execute
the tenants of 21ˢᵗ Century Leadership and Innovation. The
following are case studies that detail the ways senior leaders from
Government, Academia and Industry are driving toward 21ˢᵗ
Century Leadership and Innovation. Each leader was asked four
basic questions and their responses revel that the combination of
leadership and innovation is top of mind.

Briefly, consider the differences in the three domains.

Government Sector

Within the government sector, leaders have a deep responsibility to
the American people. As with the other sectors, a leader must have
a high degree of integrity, solid communication skills and have
energy, courage and tenacity. Leaders in the government sector can
make a difference to potentially lead change and serve in key areas
that affect millions of people to impact their quality of life. These
public service leaders have a responsibility to constituents, but

there are unique things about the public sector. In these leadership positions, you are more in the public eye; deserve greater public trust and transparency, and having to deal with the challenges of political polarization. While there are increasing demands for government services with reduced tax revenue, government at different levels have been pursuing new approaches to continue serving their constituency through innovation and service redesign of the next generation of citizen services. All this while being called on to not only makes painful choices on program cuts and creates more value from your organization.

Due to the size of the U.S. federal government, innovation requires substantive collaboration or sharing of information or processes across government bodies. An example within the U.S. Federal government is the Federal Risk and Authorization Management Program (FedRAMP). This program is an innovative policy approach to develop trusted relationships between Federal agencies and private cloud service providers. Its goal is to reduce duplicative efforts, inconsistencies and cost inefficiencies associated with the current security authorization process and allowing agencies to leverage security authorizations on a government-wide scale. Furthermore, it accelerates the adoption of cloud computing within the Federal government.

In 2012, Federal CIO Steven VanRoekel and federal CTO Todd Park launched the Presidential Innovation Fellows program that recruits top innovators and entrepreneurs from the private sector for 6-12 month "tours of duty" in government to help develop innovative solutions in areas of national significance on "high impact" federal IT projects. These initiatives range from the pre-positioning of resources for disaster response and recovery to the development of a new generation of cyber-physical "smart systems" to "Development Innovation Ventures" that will help enable the U.S. government to identify, test, and scale breakthrough solutions to the world's toughest problems.

185

The U.S. government also supports business R&D both through direct R&D funding, mostly dedicated to national-priority areas such as defense and health, and through tax incentives such as the research tax credit

Academic Sector

The synthesis of teaching and research is the fundamental basis of institutions of higher learning. In many cases, faculties do scholarly advanced scientific research, most often in association with graduate students or advanced undergraduates. Researchers spend their time writing applications for funding to do research, as well as writing scientific papers to report the findings of their research. They spend time presenting their research in oral or poster form to other scientists at group meetings, institutional meetings, and scientific conferences. This scientific research harnesses curiosity and innovation.

Leadership in academia can take many forms. The teaching aspect itself has been changing rapidly with the advent of distance learning or e-learning and the concept of a massive open online course (MOOC). A MOOC is an online course aimed at large-scale interactive student participation and open access via the Internet. Companies like Microsoft are offering grants for educators wanting to use their Windows Azure platform in their curricula. Other new cloud computing-driven innovations include the transmission of traditional academic practices (tutoring, assignments, class notices, etc.) into the cloud-based platforms for student access. Leading academic institutions are already making these changes.

More recently, cloud computing has offered attractive solutions for academic and research institutions for satisfying ad hoc needs of computing resources in research and teaching activities. Scientific and engineering research often involves the construction of mathematical and numerical models to solve complex problems that are well suited to the scalability and cost-effectiveness of cloud computing.

Other leadership is the use of university research that can lead to commercialization of IP through licensing technologies to existing companies and new University spinouts.

Public or Private Industry Sector

Public or private industry can range from small to large for-profit and publically traded companies to non-profit or charitable organizations. They may be beholden to stockholders or a single owner. Regardless of the type of industry, leaders foresee paradigm changes in society along with the continuing winds of change in the global economy. In the past, leaders could simply maintain the status quo in order to move ahead. Now new forces that range from global competition, financial pressures, to advances in technology, make it necessary to expand this narrow focus. Too often at a public company, management is mindful about bottom-line profits rather than being innovative. Consider the real question revolves not around whether a leader or management team has the vision and courage to innovate, but does the CEO have the fortitude to stand before the board and defend the opportunity to innovate and potentially fail?

Case Study: Stefanini

Stefanini: Global firm which offers consulting services, solution development and integration, Business Process Outsourcing, application and infrastructure outsourcing, and more. With support in 32 languages and the flexibility of a global company, Stefanini is focused on efficiency and meeting unique regional needs.

Industry: Information Technology

Vision / Mission:

> Vision - Be the best provider of technology, globally recognized and admired as a strategic partner, to act with passion and energy to conquer and delight customers.

> Mission - Make real the dreams of our customers, employees and shareholders through technology solutions and innovation.

Contact: Roberto Martins, Senior Executive, Chicago, IL

Q1: Compared to previous years do you find leadership changing if so why?

> Stefanini: I just think that leadership is being confused with innovation. You can lead without innovating, and you can be innovative without being a leader (which generally doesn't yield good results), so the push now (and the change) is that companies and individuals are striving to combine an innovative approach to things with classic leadership attitudes.

Q2: Are you using leadership to drive innovation in your organization? How?

> Stefanini: I don't think the type of work I do today has a lot of innovation opportunities, but I try never to get stuck with the old ways of doing things. I am using leadership to challenge the modus operandi, which is how.

Q3: What challenges prevent you from leading with innovation in mind?

> Stefanini: The same processes, rules, standards that were created somewhere during the late 90's, early 2000's, that are still in place in many companies. Companies that have not embraced the BYOD wave, the flexible work schedule, the work x life balance, usually stifle innovation leadership with their set ways.

Q4: What do you anticipate the future results will be from the relationship between leadership and innovation?

> Stefanini: I think we still cannot teach people to be leaders. We can hone skills of born leaders, but not create them. I believe the focus will be on teaching the leaders to be creative, and that can be more easily achieved, in my opinion. I actually tend to think that GOOD leaders are born creative people as well. It is a symbiotic relationship.

Case Study: Appleby & Associates

Appleby & Associates: Provide multi-talented consultants who fit the culture of the organization; bring the right evidenced-based methods and tools to the table; empower our clients to succeed long after we have finished our work.

Industry: Consulting

Vision / Mission:

Appleby & Associates is an alliance of organization development consultants, specializing in building workplaces where people fully commit their talents to making their organization and customers successful. We bring, individually and collectively, a reputation for excellence and a passion for bringing out the best in an organization and its people. We help leaders and change agents envision, design, build, and sustain great organizations.

Contact: John Gattasse, Practice Leader – Aerospace

John Gattasse is Practice Leader in Aerospace at Appleby & Associates. Appleby & Associates is an alliance of organization and business development consultants. Prior to this he was Managing Director of Corporate Sales and Market Development at the American Institute of Aeronautics and Astronautics, the world's largest technical and professional membership society. He also served as Vice President of Sales and Marketing at Meggitt, a global engineering group specializing in extreme environment products and smart sub-systems for aerospace, defense and energy markets. He had Management responsibility for the sales & marketing team at Securaplane Technologies, a division of Meggitt. Mr. Gattasse was Director of Global Engine Development at TIMET, where he led business development activities by identifying, prioritizing and coordinating cross functional efforts to capture targeted opportunities aligned with TIMET's aerospace strategy.

Previously he worked for Rolls Royce as Director Airline Sales, Director CorporateCare and serving finally as a Business Development Executive. He served as Director Commercial and as Product Manager for TRW Aeronautical (currently an UTC company and formerly Goodrich and Lucas Aerospace). Mr. Gattasse holds a Master of Business Administration in Economics from Saint John's University and a Bachelor of Arts in Economics from Queens College, both in New York.

Q1: Compared to previous years do you find leadership changing if so why?

> Appleby & Associates: Absolutely. I've recently seen a shift to the servant leadership style in several large corporations in the aerospace industry. The servant leader tends to be more concerned about his/her team and displays a higher dose of humility. That combined with the will-to-succeed is a powerful combination for success.

Q2: Are you using leadership to drive innovation in your organization? How?

> Appleby & Associates: Constantly. A strong leadership style coupled with continuous improvement naturally drives innovation along with other lean processes. The leader of the organization inspires the team and calls for action, setting direction and providing support. The team then innovates through established processes using their own creativity and expertise.

Q3: What challenges prevent you from leading with innovation in mind?

> Appleby & Associates: The business leader is faced with realities that can delay innovative projects such as a lack of cash flow and other priorities i.e. existing contracts or retention efforts. Nevertheless, innovation is always at the center of every growth strategy and shouldn't be discarded in the business plan.

Q4: What do you anticipate the future results will be from the relationship between leadership and innovation?

Appleby & Associates: The results of this dynamic combination between leadership and innovation are simply sustained growth, which is what most businesses are striving for. Once you have fine-tuned your processes and established a winning strategy, the business will benefit from sustained growth over the long-term.

Case Study: PBS Marketing/Federal Concierge LLC

PBS Marketing / Federal Concierge LLC: Federal Concierge now provides consulting support in the areas of Capital Planning, Investment Control, Exhibit 300 support, Acquisition; Program Management; Enterprise Architecture; Alternative Analysis; Risk Management; Performance Improvement; Security and Privacy; GAO-compliant Life-Cycle Cost Estimation / Formulation, IT Assessments, Independent Verification & Validation (IV&V).

Industry: Government Marketing / Education / Consulting

Vision / Mission:
> The Federal Concierge service is an on-call service for businesses providing or selling – or who want to provide and sell – to the Federal Government.

Contact: Janelle Moore, President, PBS Marketing/ Federal Concierge LLC
> Janelle Moore is the President and lead consultant of a woman-owned small business that provides professional services in the areas of Information Technology and Financial Management to the federal government and other contracting firms specializing in the government. Janelle leads a virtual concierge staff as well as directly supports a portfolio of federal clients and contracting firms as a subject matter expert in federal budgeting and capital investment planning.

Q1: Compared to previous years do you find leadership changing if so why?
> PBS Marketing/ Federal Concierge LLC: In Government, I do see leadership changing due to budget constraints imposed by continuing resolutions, furloughs and sequestration. Leadership, both in government, and for those contracting firms supporting the government, are forced to make resource decisions and operate in extremely tight fiscal constraints.

Q2: Are you using leadership to drive innovation in your organization? How?

> PBS Marketing/ Federal Concierge LLC: Yes. In my company, Federal Concierge LLC, we are using leadership to mandate that our teams be able to use the cloud for nearly all of our IT Functions, enabling our staff to be more virtually located, virtually accessible and efficient with response times both to other members of our team as well as clients. By creating the IT policies at the top, and by outsourcing nearly all of our IT functions, we have streamlined our organization, our overhead costs and our staff resource costs.

Q3: What challenges prevent you from leading with innovation in mind?

> PBS Marketing/ Federal Concierge LLC: There is always a bottleneck somewhere. Sometimes it's resistance to change, or finding that an IT Service provider can't deliver contractually on what was sold as a scalable IT solution, so we have to work to identify those costs quickly and respond; maintaining a workable alternatives analysis with fresh data has allowed us to amputate bottleneck challenges and the costs that are incurred and move rapidly to an alternate solution. The range of Cloud and IT Services has allowed us to overcome those challenges rapidly once we diagnose them.

Q4: What do you anticipate the future results will be from the relationship between leadership and innovation?

> PBS Marketing/ Federal Concierge LLC: I don't think the leader has to be the innovator, but the leader must be able to recognize the innovative minds on the team and leverage those folks for the assets they can be as problem solvers, and they need to be able to select innovative ideas that bring a balance between improvement and risk. Leaders who can recognize innovation and move ahead rapidly will be able to maximize on profitability, strategic position in a market, and potential growth.

Case Study: United Negro College Fund (UNCF)

United Negro College Fund (UNCF): The United Negro College Fund (UNCF) is a nonprofit organization dedicated to increasing the numbers of African-Americans going to college and completing their college education. The UNCF has recently launched an initiative focused on building infrastructure and capacity for innovation and tech-entrepreneurship at historically black colleges and universities.

Industry: Education

Vision / Mission:

UNCF's vision is to significantly increase the numbers of African-Americans pursuing college and advanced degrees, and to transform historically black colleges and universities into nodes and hubs of innovation and entrepreneurship.

Contact: Chad Womack, PhD, United Negro College Fund (UNCF): Chad Womack, PhD is the National Director, STEM Initiatives - UNCF-Merck Fellowship Program and the HBCU Center for Innovation, Commercialization and Entrepreneurship (ICE).

Q1: Compared to previous years do you find leadership changing if so why?

United Negro College Fund (UNCF): Yes. Leadership models are changing within organizational hierarchies to be more inclusive, flattened and horizontal (less vertical). This opens the opportunity for greater collaborative and partnership driven efforts within the organization.

Q2: Are you using leadership to drive innovation in your organization? How?

United Negro College Fund (UNCF): Yes. By identifying opportunities to leverage existing assets within the organization including social capital that can be invested in establishing and building relationships with other entities interested in driving similar outcomes and impacts.

Q3: What challenges prevent you from leading with innovation in mind?

United Negro College Fund (UNCF): Existing organizational structures, organograms and methodologies that are outdated.

Q4: What do you anticipate the future results will be from the relationship between leadership and innovation?

United Negro College Fund (UNCF): Leadership will drive innovation in organizational processes and vision, and leverage organizational assets to increase the organization's value proposition as a key intermediary stakeholder in the higher education landscape.

Case Study: White House HBCU STEM and Innovation Committee

The National Science and Technology Council (NSTC) was established by Executive Order on November 23, 1993. This Cabinet-level council is the principal body within the executive branch that coordinates science and technology policy across the diverse entities that make up the Federal research and development enterprise. Chaired by the President, the membership of the NSTC consists of the Vice President, the Director of the Office of Science and Technology Policy, Cabinet Secretaries and Agency Heads with significant science and technology responsibilities, and other White House officials.

The NSTC is organized into five primary committees: Science, Technology, Engineering, and Mathematics (STEM) Education; Science; Technology; Environment, Natural Resources and Sustainability; and Homeland and National Security. Each of these committees oversees subgroups focused on different aspects of science and technology. One of the NSTC's primary objectives is to establish clear national goals for Federal science and technology investments in an array of areas that span virtually all the mission areas of the executive branch. The Council prepares coordinated interagency research and development strategies to form investment packages that are aimed at achieving multiple national goals.

Industry: Government

Vision / Mission:
>The National Science and Technology Council Committee on STEM Education (CoSTEM) coordinates Federal programs and activities in support of STEM education pursuant to the requirements of Sec. 101 of the America COMPETES Reauthorization Act of 2010. The CoSTEM addresses education and workforce policy issues; research and development efforts that focus on STEM education at the PreK-12, undergraduate, graduate, and lifelong learning

levels; and current and projected STEM workforce needs, trends, and issues. The CoSTEM performs three functions: review and assessment of Federal STEM education activities and programs; with the Office of Management and Budget, coordination of STEM education activities and programs across Federal agencies; and development and implementation of a 5-Year Federal STEM education strategic plan through the participating agencies, to be updated every five years.

Contact: Kenneth S. Tolson, Sr.

Kenneth S. Tolson, Sr. is a Strategic technology leader and subject matter expert for the Obama Administration and key developer of the "Cloud-First" policy for HBCUs. He served as subject matter expert on the design of the first Federal IT Dashboard, which lead to the development of the first HBCU dashboard. Working with the Federal CIO and CTO, led efforts within Executive Office of the President (EOP) to help build a coalition to adopt and establish Data.gov initiative across the EOP enterprise to track IT investments within the various agencies. Ken introduced the HBCU community to the transformational power of cloud computing and established cross-functional working groups to assess infrastructure and resources to implement the first HBCU cloud. As chairman of the STEM, Innovation and technology committee he has been charged with and successful in cutting waste, strengthening cyber security and building an open and transparent educational government resources through technology and enhancing STEM and Innovation opportunities across the HBCU enterprise. Subject matter expert working with the WH EOP to manage a broad policy portfolio focusing on both the digital and social media, IT and Innovation across the federal agencies to improve economic opportunity for all.

Q1: Compared to previous years do you find leadership changing if so why?

Yes, Leadership styles are changing and attitudes about poor leadership and becoming more impactful.

Q2: Are you using leadership to drive innovation in your organization? How?

Yes, we are working to leverage new technologies to drive innovation. Our focus on metrics is helping us to gain insight on what works and what doesn't.

Q3: What challenges prevent you from leading with innovation in mind?

Budget constraints, rate of change across the education vertical and inability to communicate need for innovation culture are key challenges.

Q4: What do you anticipate the future results will be from the relationship between leadership and innovation?

Growth of diverse organizations that focus on the modern leadership model detailed in this book.

Case Study: RONIN Information Technology Services LLC

RONIN Information Technology Services, LLC: RONIN Information Technology Services, LLC, is a minority and veteran-owned professional services company that provide business process re-engineering, program management and IT management consulting services to clients in the federal marketplace. RONIN IT Services helps government clients reduce overall costs and improve program success through efficient business process transformation and integration of disparate services and technologies.

Industry: Government Information Technology

Vision / Mission:

> RONIN IT Services' unique blend of business process re-engineering, program management and management consulting services provides customers with the most robust and cost effective solutions in the industry. We believe that our experience, integrity and legacy of satisfaction, coupled with our agility and understanding of customer needs uniquely qualify us as the partner for the future.

Contact: Kevin Manuel-Scott, Chairman and CEO, RONIN IT Services

Q1: Compared to previous years do you find leadership changing if so why?

> RONIN IT Services: I think leaders evolve as their experiences increase. Much like a Navy Captain starts out as an Ensign, over time, they are groomed into the leader ultimately responsible for a base or an afloat command. I believe leadership in business has changed only in that the expectations for success have changed. I have seen organizations whose leaders are expected to be proverbial "rain makers" appeasing shareholder and investors desires for immediate, sustainable, double-digit profits and return on investments. Many leaders have been successful, but at

significant cost to the morale of their organizations. Coining the late Steve Jobs, leaders should "Think Different!" I am hopeful that business leaders will continue changing when innovation trumps the desire for immediate profits, when leaders can go against the grain for the morale of the organization, and collaboration with winners becomes the standard.

Q2: Are you using leadership to drive innovation in your organization? How?

RONIN IT Services: At RONIN IT Services, we execute on a clearly defined strategic plan, which articulates our mission and vision, and allows us to enhance our innovation strategy for the future. We incorporate not only what our customers want today, but also what they want to be in the future. Through business process innovation and transformation, we help our customers focus on an offensive posture versus a defensive posture in cyber security. We develop tools and technologies as well as implement services that enable our customers to respond to threats more rapidly.

Q3: What challenges prevent you from leading with innovation in mind?

RONIN IT Services: We experience challenges in access to working capital to enhance our research and development capabilities in business transformation through cyber defense and exploitation. We are able to mitigate these challenges through partnerships with academic institutions whose focus is development of exploitation and adversarial strategies in cyber defense. We also collaborate with members of various hacker communities to develop techniques not often found in traditional environments.

Q4: What do you anticipate the future results will be from the relationship between leadership and innovation?

RONIN IT Services: In my Global Sales Institute class at Electronic Data Systems (EDS) Corporation (now HP), the key question I learned to always ask a client in context is, "why are you changing the way you're doing business?" What I have come to learn from that question is clients seek ways to reduce their overall costs, create greater efficiencies, and ultimately transform their businesses. Sometimes clients want the status quo, other times they want innovation which will lead to reduced costs, greater efficiencies and business transformation. It is industries responsibility to convey an innovative way forward for customer to achieve their goals. The late Steve Jobs helped write the text for the "Think Different" ads: "Here's to the crazy ones. The misfits. The rebels. The troublemakers. The round pegs in the square holes…" Steve Jobs bucked traditional systems and attitudes, resulting in the world being a different…better place. I anticipate the future results from the relationship between leadership and innovation to increase so long as leaders are willing to think outside the box and don't settle for mediocrity.

Part 3:
Bring the Future Back

The Real Magic is pulling the
Future Back to the Present

—Haden Land

Chapter Ten

Creating the Future Leadership and Innovation Engine

*The greatest danger for most of us is not
that our aim is too high and we miss it,
but that it is too low and we reach it*

—Michelangelo

Science Technology Engineering & Math (STEM)

United States leadership, economic competitiveness and growth tomorrow depend on how we educate our students today, especially in the fields of Science, Technology, Engineering and Math (STEM). Concern for the nation's economic competitiveness and the related need for education programs in support of future generations are not new. Major reports and studies over the last several years have brought the need for comprehensive STEM education into clear focus.

STEM related fields are many and diverse. STEM disciplines, as identified by the National Science Foundation (NSF) are based on a broad definition that includes: Agricultural Sciences, Biological Sciences, Chemistry, Computer and Information Technology Sciences, economics and other natural and social/behavioral sciences Engineering, Geosciences, Life Sciences, Mathematics, physical sciences (physics & astronomy), Psychology, Social Sciences), science, and earth atmospheric & ocean sciences. Many organizations in the United States follow the NSF guidelines.

President Barack Obama has championed the cause and in November 2009 launched the Educate to Innovate campaign to improve the participation and performance of America's students in STEM. (Remarks by the President on the "Educate to Innovate" Campaign, 2010) This campaign includes education reform not only from the federal government but also enlists leading companies, foundations, non-profits, universities, and science and engineering professional organizations to work with young people across America to excel in science and math. The initial commitment from the private sector to this campaign has exceeded $260 million and is expected to grow.

In a national poll conducted by the Pew Research Center and Smithsonian magazine, when asked the key reason young people don't pursue degrees in science and math, 22 percent of those surveyed said such degrees weren't useful to their careers and 20 percent said the subjects were "too boring." The most common response was that science and math were "too hard," a belief held by 46 percent of respondents.

While supporters of STEM education warn that U.S. students are falling behind other nations in technical subjects, the reality is somewhat different. In this same survey, respondents tended to rank American youths as poor in contrast to other nations. On a standardized Program for International Student Assessment (PISA) science test, 15-year olds in the United States, ranked in the middle, scoring 17th out of the 34 developed nations in 2009, the most recent year for which results are available. (How much to Americans know about Science, 2013)

In a 2007 U.S. Department of Labor STEM Workforce Challenge Report (Labor, 2007), several key statistics and estimates are brought forward that signify the importance of STEM as critical engines of innovation and growth:

- Scientific innovation has produced roughly half of all U.S. economic growth in the last 50 years. (National Science Foundation 2004).

- While only about five percent of the U.S. workforce is employed in STEM fields, the STEM workforce accounts for more than fifty percent of the nation's sustained economic growth. (Babco 2004).

- An Educational Testing Service survey, 61 percent of opinion leaders and 40 percent of the general public identify math, science and technology skills as the most important ingredients in the nation's strategy to compete in the global economy. (Zinth 2006).

- The Business Roundtable (2005) warns that, if current trends continue, more than 90 percent of all scientists and engineers in the world will live in Asia.

In October 2005, National Academies, in response to a bipartisan request by members of the US Senate and House of Representatives, issued a report titled Rising Above the Gathering Storm: Energizing and Employing America for a Brighter Economic Future stating that "America is in substantial danger of losing its economic leadership position and suffering a concomitant decline in the standard of living of its citizens because of a looming inability to compete in the global marketplace". The report issued a call to strengthen K-12 education and double the federal basic-research budget.

In 2007 Congress passed the America COMPETES Act, which authorized many recommendations from the Gathering Storm report. But most of the Act's measures went unfunded until the stimulus package was passed early in 2009, a package that increased total federal funding for K-12 education, provided scholarships for future math and science teachers, and funded the Advanced Research Projects Agency-Energy, which is dedicated to supporting transformational basic research on energy.

A subsequent 2010 report, Rising Above the Gathering Storm, Revisited was issued that provides a snapshot of the activities of the government and the private sector in the past five years. It provided an analysis of how the original recommendations have or have not been acted upon and their related consequences on future competitiveness. This report is a wake-up call about the state of science and innovation in America with the unanimous view of the authors concluding that our nation's competitive outlook has worsened. Other nations have been markedly progressing, thereby affecting America's relative ability to compete for new factories, research laboratories, and jobs. These reports collectively show that trends in K-12 along with higher education science and math preparation, coupled with demographic and labor supply trends, point to a serious challenge for the United States. "The Gathering Storm effort once again finds itself at a tipping point," said Norman R. Augustine, one of the new report's authors and chair of the original Gathering Storm committee. He further stated, "Addressing America's competitiveness challenge will require many years if not decades". (Rising above the Gathering Storm, Revisited, 2010) This report, in addition to the original *Gathering Storm* volume, provides the roadmap to meet that goal.

The report notes many indications that the United States' competitive capacity is slipping, including the following:

- In 2009, 51 percent of U.S. patents were awarded to non-U.S. companies.

- China has replaced the U.S. as the world's number one high-technology exporter and is now second in the world in publication of biomedical research articles.

- Between 1996 and 1999, 157 new drugs were approved in the United States. In a corresponding period 10 years later, the number dropped to 74.

- Almost one-third of U.S. manufacturing companies responding to a recent survey say they are suffering from some level of skills shortage.

- According to the ACT College Readiness Report, 78 percent of U.S. high school graduates in 2008 did not meet readiness benchmark levels for one or more entry-level college courses in mathematics, science, reading, and English
- The World Economic Forum ranks the U.S. 48th in the quality of its math and science education.

The study further states that without a serious response, "the U.S. will lose quality jobs to other nations, lowering our standard of living, reducing tax revenues, and weakening the domestic market for goods and services. Once this cycle accelerates, it will be difficult to regain lost preeminence in technology driven innovation and its economic benefits".

While the number of U.S. undergraduate degrees being awarded in most STEM disciplines (science, technology, engineering and math) has been rising steadily, some American employers say they are having trouble finding qualified candidates to fill jobs in those disciplines. According to Nicole Smith, senior economist at the Georgetown University Center on Education and the Workforce, this mismatch is occurring based on people with STEM degrees choosing careers in other fields due to higher perceived status, greater potential for management or simply higher pay. "Biology students become doctors; math majors go into finance," she explains.

Smith further believes that several steps could make STEM jobs more attractive to students such as raising salaries in certain disciplines could help. Starting wages in computer science and engineering have increased steadily over time, for example, but wages in biology have not. She also states that this mismatch is not occurring because of an actual shortage of graduates as the numbers of job openings and new degree holders align fairly closely or that more foreign-born students are returning home after earning U.S. degrees. (Fischetti, 2012)

However, despite all of the dire projections and statistics, there are those that believe that the STEM issues are overblown. In a Scientific American article Beryl Lieff Benderly, a fellow of the American Association for the Advancement of Science, argues that the U.S. educational system actually produces too many qualified researchers for too few positions, particularly in academia. (Benderly, 2010)

Regardless, which camp that you're in, here are some recent statistics show the importance and value of STEM-based education:

- According to the U.S. Bureau of Statistics, in the next five years, STEM jobs are projected to grow twice as quickly as jobs in other fields. While all jobs are expected to grow by 10.4%, STEM jobs are expected to increase by 21.4%. Similarly, 80% of jobs in the next decade will require technical skills.

- The US Department of Labor claims that out of the 20 fastest growing occupations projected to 2014, 15 of them require significant mathematics or science preparation. The U.S. will have over 1 million job openings in STEM-related fields by 2018; yet, according to the U.S. Bureau of Statistics, only 16% of U.S. bachelor's degrees will specialize in STEM. As a nation, the United States is not graduating nearly enough STEM majors to supply the demand.

- From another perspective, of the 3.8 million 9th graders in the US, only 233,000 end up choosing a STEM degree in college (National Center for Education Statistics). That means only six STEM graduates out of every 100 9th graders. (The STEM Dilemma)

The United States needs to pay more attention to technical education to prepare tomorrow's workforce and to stimulate interest in the sciences. One approach is making science jobs appear more exciting would also improve their attractiveness and would finding ways to get society to hold STEM professions in higher regard. Surveys of graduating STEM students show that they value social "recognition" and that they think society holds professionals such as doctors and corporate executives in higher esteem than scientists or engineers. Reaching students at a young age in terms of making the students interested in studying STEM related fields has to start early. It is also important to make sure that students are clear about what career path they're at least interested in when they get into college.

There is a new movement championed by Rhode Island School of Design (RISD) that incorporates Art into STEM.

STEM + Art = STEAM

The objectives of the STEAM movement are to:

- transform research policy to place Art + Design at the center of STEM
- encourage integration of Art + Design in K–20 education
- influence employers to hire artists and designers to drive innovation

This is based on the premise that arts education is a key to creativity, and creativity is an essential component of, and spurs innovation.

How Leadership affects STEM / STEAM

The United States needs to pay more attention to technical education to prepare tomorrow's workforce and to stimulate interest in the sciences.

Today's leaders need to stand up and serve as role models to encourage school students to develop the critical skills needed for the competitive workforce of tomorrow. There is the need to be more aggressive in highlighting stories of successful leaders in STEM professions.

On a personal level, encourage a student to consider a STEM career. This might be a family member or that of a colleague. Deeper personal involvement includes becoming a math or science tutor at a local school.

At a group or corporate level, an approach is for a core of respected business leaders to form a STEM initiative within a school district. These are individuals who understand the feasibility of and be knowledgeable advocates of a STEM education. A good example is the Mobile Alabama based Engaging Youth through Engineering (EYE) program. EYE is a workforce and economic development initiative created to bring relevance to the K-12 mathematics and science curriculum. The goal of EYE is to inspire, engage and prepare middle school students to take the coursework needed to support the growing demand for highly skilled and technology-savvy workers for major industries located in the Mobile, Alabama area, including aerospace and shipbuilding. Students at all levels in the EYE initiative - elementary, middle, and high school - use an Engineering Design Process to solve real-world engineering challenges. (Mobile area education foundation, n.d.)

This program can be furthered by business leaders persuading their organizations to partner with schools with the aim at improving math and science education for thousands of high-need public schools. General Electric's outreach to the Chicago Hispanic community is one example. (www.reuters.com, 2013) In this initiative, students had the opportunity to tour a business fair and see firsthand the various STEM-related industries in which GE is involved. GE executives held a roundtable discussion with students; sharing the steps they took to build their careers and some of the lessons they learned along the way.

For those that are teachers and educators, leadership also plays an important role as education leaders that are positioned to influence school policies and practices, student achievement, as well as fellow education professionals.

Consider creating internship programs, summer jobs and programs for students to work within your organization.

Events such as the annual USA Science & Engineering Festival is part of a national grassroots effort to advance STEM education and inspires the next generation of scientists and engineers with hands-on experiences of understanding and solving difficult problems. (USAScienceFestival.org, 2013) The events' exhibitors, performers, speakers, partners, sponsors and advisors are a who-is-who of science and engineering in the United States: from major academic centers and leading research institutes and government agencies to cutting-edge high tech companies, museums and community organizations. The USA Science & Engineering Festival, as the country's only national science festival, was developed to encourage youth to pursue careers in science and engineering by celebrating science in much the same way as would celebrate Hollywood celebrities, professional athletes and pop stars.

Leaders need to develop a strategy for building a flexible workforce that is based upon the deep technical skills that are rooted in STEM disciplines.

Generational Differences

At a meeting with your team, ask the following question: Do you remember when Kennedy died? The responses may vary from the more senior members of you team saying "assassinated in Dallas" to younger members stating "plane crash going to Martha's Vineyard" to the latest generation saying "Who?"

It's not uncommon to find different generations that span almost 50 years in an organization today.

This point out a diversity issue that needs to be recognized and understood, being that of generational differences. Different generations have rather different attitudes, values, beliefs social and economic views, religious beliefs, motivations, and technological influences from one another. A lack of understanding regarding generational differences from a wide range of age groups contributes to conflict within an organization resulting in strained working relationships, misunderstanding, miscommunications, lower productivity, and increased turnover. Also consider that leadership style varies among generations and has potential impact on overall organizational success.

There are four generational groups in the workplace today: "The Greatest Generation" or "Traditionals", (born 1924 to 1943); "Baby Boomers" (born 1944 to 1963), "Generation X" (born 1964 to 1983), and finally "Generation Y" or "Millenials" (born 1984 to 2000).

Consider the following:

- Traditionalists respond to a leadership modeled in a command-and-control structured top-down hierarchy. They are survivors of hard times having gone through world wars and difficult financial times. Traditionalists are considered to be loyal and self-sacrificing, and are probably the least comfortable with new technology.

- The Baby Boomers are sometimes called the "Me Generation" because they tend to focus more on their own well being, rather than the group. They are hard working, competitive, and motivated by power, position, perks and prestige.

- Gen X tends to be less hierarchical, more casual about authority, and exhibit more independence than its predecessor generations. They are focused on learning, generally better educated with a higher percentage of college graduates and have a strong work/ life balance structure. But Gen X tend to be less optimistic and don't believe that they will be as well off as their parents' generation.

- Large numbers of Generation Y are now entering the workforce. This generation grew up with access to technology from birth. They tend to be less disciplined than previous generations, and have the need to know why they're doing what they're doing. Based on their use of social media, they tend to have shorter attention spans, be more sociable and collaborate more in small groups. They have a greater appreciation of diversity and like informality. Generation Y has been found to be missing communication skills and don't appear to have the work ethic of previous generations. Typically leaders basically lead, apply techniques, and communication styles to those of the same generation that they are a part of and most comfortable with. Having everyone conform to your style and preferences will not work. Demonstrate leadership by bringing generations together for a common purpose. While the Boomers "lived to work", the Gen Y "work to live." Traditionalists are very structured and require clear rules and boundaries while Gen X are informal, require freedom and lots of feedback at regular intervals. Even communications preferences exist with Boomers preferring personal or phone conversations or paper memos, Gen X favoring emails, and Gen Y doing texts.

Traditionalists	Boomers	Gen-X	Gen-Y
1900-1945	1946-1964	1965-1980	1981-1999
Respect Authority Highly Structured Stable Hardworking Loyal Reluctant to Change	Questions Authority Strong Work Ethic	Work-Life Balance More Social Not as Loyal Embraces Diversity Lesser Work Ethic	Embraces Diversity Collective Values Less Process Focused

Generational Differences

Typically leaders basically lead, apply techniques, and communication styles to those of the same generation that they are a part of and most comfortable with. Having everyone conform to your style and preferences will not work. Demonstrate leadership by bringing generations together for a common purpose. While the Boomers lived to work, the Gen Y work to live. Traditionalists are very structured and require clear rules and boundaries while Gen X are informal, require freedom and lots of feedback at regular intervals. Even communications preferences exist with Boomers preferring personal or phone conversations or paper memos, Gen X favoring emails, and Gen Y doing texts. Familiarity with technology varies by generation. Additionally technology awareness and knowledge also varies by job function and the extent to which the technology is used to perform their functions.

Consider collaboration. The sharing of knowledge and ideas are dependent upon the generation. For example, the baby boomer generation sees "knowledge as power" that needs to be protected and divulged only as required. Generation X and Y view knowledge that is something to be shared with everyone, as evidenced by their use of social media. Teams are very important to developing and nurturing innovation that should include people who will challenge the status quo or reluctant to share knowledge.

If you lead a Gen-X or Gen-Y individual that is particularly talented and you want to ensure that he or she stays within the organization, note that these two generations have the traits of building portable careers to remain flexible.

Leading multi-generational individuals is akin to herding cats. But each generation has its own requirements that must be met with a flexible leadership style. Consider such leadership styles as:

- Creating a work environment conducive for each generation
- Delegating work that involves the strengths of each generation
- Coach and mentor team members individually
- Customizing communication based on their preferences

Do you take into account these generational differences in your leadership style?

Impact of Gamification

While the word gamification has only recently emerged, the underlying concepts are based on Human Computer Interaction (HCI). Gamification is basically the process of taking the engagement mechanisms and tactics we find in games and incorporating them into ordinary activities to provoke a deeper user experience, engagement and dedication. As the influence of the games culture and social media continues to expand, organizations are increasingly beginning to turn to gamification to maintain user engagement and provide an innovative method to help solve problems or task activities.

It's no longer sufficient for organizations to have a simple static informational website, blogs, posts on Facebook or to send tweets to engage with end users. More interactive and creative methods for a sustained two-way dialog need to be applied to maintain and cultivate user interest. The use of smart phones and mobile computing devices, now provide the tools to better facilitate this exchange.

The need for engagement and motivation in a social setting drew on the popularity of on-line gaming to incorporate game techniques into social media. The gamification model is considered by some to be an offshoot of Crowd sourcing as it offers a strategy for influencing and motivating the behavior of people

Gamification is defined as the use of game techniques, design principles and systems to make business activities more entertaining and engaging to an end user. The goal is to motivate and influence individuals or groups to drive behaviors and result in desired outcomes. Note that applying gamification to an application does not result in a game. The intent is for users not to realize that they are playing a game.

The science behind gamification as its being applied to Crowd sourcing and other Social Media models is to make the performance of an otherwise routine online task, something entertaining and potentially rewarding for the user. The intent is to motivate the user through the introduction of a competitive dynamic where tasks are incorporated as actions within a game. Dynamics are the time-based patterns and systems in the game.

As depicted in Figure 11, gamification is the blend of loyalty & rewards programs, user engagement, social behavior and game design.

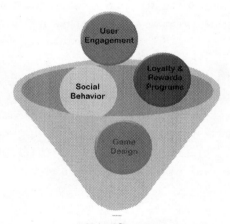

Gamification

Loyalty & Rewards Program

A loyalty & rewards program is a plan designed to lower the turnover among users of a product or service by rewarding them with certain benefits for remaining involved. In a business setting, traditional loyalty programs might automatically award points based on concrete user consumption (frequent flyer airline miles or dollars spent). These programs typically allow users to accumulate points to open up new levels of membership. In a gamification-based system, a user is drawn in through the game dynamics with potential variable and unpredictable reinforcement and rewards.

Rewards and incentives are deeply embedded in everything we do as humans. The options for presenting a range of digital rewards include motivational triggers such as: positive feedback; virtual good & services; leader boards; noticeable advancement through the "game" upon successfully performing the work (e.g. progression to a new level or different storyline); some form of non-monetary or monetary recognition (the awarding points, badges, and status levels that represent various levels of achievement). The rewards and recognition mechanism should match level of difficulty so users achieve a sense of accomplishment.

User Engagement

Engagement is the action of occupying, attracting or involving a user's attention that balance skill and challenge that provides a good UX (User Experience) and sense of accomplishment. From a business perspective, engagement marketing is a strategy of encouraging the involvement and participation of consumers in a relevant area for the purposes of influencing brand or product awareness. For gamification, effective engagement requires relevant content or storyline to provide an effective journey through the game. The journey of a user's experience or progression over time through the game is known as the lifecycle. Depending on the storyline, the lifecycle may involve an orderly progression through game levels from novice / beginner to master / expert. A component of the user engagement is to make sure that they continue to remain engaged. A good example is Zynga's Farmville whereby if the user does not actively return to their virtual farm frequently, the crops that they have planted and nurtured will begin to die with any rewards and status gained being lost.

Social Behavior

Social Behavior is comprised of the actions or reactions of a person in response to external or internal stimuli. In the case of gamification, it is how users connect, engage, share and react with other users.

Game Design

The user of a gamified application is typically a consumer of a product or service. A great game, regardless of the scenario, should have a goal, some challenges and some reward. However, it also needs to be readily understandable and simple enough to use by a wide audience. The mechanics of the game are the features that make user progress visible. Certain patterns are programmed into games such as rewards and incentive schedules, and surprises.

A point to consider is that by the time the average American turns 21, they will have spent more than 10,000 hours playing games [1]. This brings up an important aspect to gamification as that young people in the marketplace or entering the workforce have been raised with video games as a form of entertainment. Their expectation is for continuous incremental reinforcement and action when on-line or at work.

Cloud computing, mobile devices and gamification can be considered to be game changers. There are several key areas where gamification functionality is amplified through the use of the cloud-computing ecosystem.

Gamification elements can be delivered via Software as a Service (SaaS). The SaaS elements can include any of the gamification elements that include the game engine, loyalty / reward management, user engagement, data tabulation and aggregation components.

An example of the applicability of cloud computing is the ability to readily support hundreds of thousands of players simultaneously in Massively Multiplayer Online Games (MMOG). Cloud computing creates an elastic hardware / software solution that can expand and contract to meet the demand of any gamified environment, be it the number of users or platform requirements and resources. Another key aspect is the "pay-per-use" subscription model where the users only pay for the resources that they consume.

Some basic gamification techniques began appearing several years ago in Smart phone apps and browser-based enterprise applications that were used to improve user and employee engagement. Today's generation is increasingly tied to mobile devices and is beginning to utilize their own personally owned devices at work as a BYOD (Bring-Your-Own-Device).

With the advent of the new Hypertext Markup Language release 5 (HTML5) web standards, the trend to incorporate gamification functionality in mobile app design will only increase. Through the use of the capabilities provided by HTML5, it is now possible to develop platform independent applications that can be accessed by any device with a compatible web browser that supports HTML5 features. Through this platform independence, a developer should be able to write code once and have it execute in variety of devices including PCs and Mobile devices (Android, iOS, Windows Mobile, etc.). Other key elements that distinguish HTML5 as a strong platform for gamification includes:

- New parallel processing capabilities that enable an application to spawn background JavaScript threads / tasks that execute in parallel to the main page. This feature is important for CPU intensive applications such as animations and leverages the multi-core capabilities in current CPUs

- The ability to build animations and graphics through APIs that create and manipulate 2D shapes and bitmap images. Further advanced graphics capabilities are available as CSS3 (Cascading Style Sheet) 3, provides a built-in solution to create 3D graphics with 3D transformations

- The ability of an application to work off-line when disconnected from the Internet and synchronize once reconnected through the use of application data caching. This feature enables an application to store data locally and therefore reduces the number of server-side requests each time a page loads or data usage from the cloud

An organization can now incorporate game methods into their application through cloud-based plug-and-play integration. Several of the many gamification companies that have emerged recently include Badgerville, Bunchball, and Manumatix.

Organizations are beginning to realize that gamification is a strategic engagement model. People need reward, status, achievement, competition and self-expression in their lives.

In 2011, the Gartner IT research organization made two significant statements regarding gamification [2]. The first is that gamification is deemed significant enough to be on the Gartner's Hype Cycle chart, an info graphic designed to show the potential real-world success of this emerging technology. The second is their prediction that "by 2015, more than 50 percent of organizations that manage innovation processes will gamify those processes".

Business value and innovation through gamification can come in many forms.

Enterprise level Crowd sourcing firms, such as CrowdFlower, use some game mechanics to have users perform real work through the completion of trivial web-based tasks. Depending on the business model, Crowd Sourcing users may receive financial remuneration for their work activity.

Closely associated to Crowd Sourcing is the concept of micro tasking, which is the outsourcing of tasks to crowds or workers. Micro tasking has taken may forms but are generally smaller projects or offshoots of larger projects. Both Crowd Sourcing and micro tasking can unleash the talents and energies of people to solve problems and complete tasks of varying size.

In Digitalkoot, which is described in further detail in the next section, users play actual computer games with useful micro tasks being a side product. In this particular case no financial rewards are provided.

The confluence of Crowd Sourcing and gamification can create a competitive game-like setting to any innovative non-game business models to aid in solving complex problems [e.g., Foldit], the gathering of data from the public about on-going or past events [e.g., StreetViolence.org], or collect recommendations or ideas [e.g., IdeaStreet].

Some of the basic areas where gamification concepts can be incorporated are

- Marketing a product or service
- Customer relations
- Motivation and competition
- User engagement for Crowd sourcing
- Enlivening and communicating topics, which are considered dull
- Topic areas where it is difficult to engage users
- Training or interactive learning sessions

A side benefit of gamification is the generation of and access to valuable customer activity data. As with all data collected and aggregated from individuals, there is the privacy aspect to contend with and there may be significant marketing value associated with it. Gamification is assuming core-underlying roles in numerous business customer, social media, or employee-facing applications as noted in the following examples:

Banking and Financial Management

Financial institutions' key goals are to provide a more engaging customer experience and reward its online banking users for changing their spending habits and better managing their personal finances. While the financial industry has been slow in recognizing the value of gamification, a European bank that is part of the IND group, has launched new services that have a gamification core.

Healthcare

Healthcare and fitness applications can make health related activities and treatments something that people like to do rather than something they should do. Gamification can help solve health related problems relating to adherence to medication, management of chemotherapy treatment, smoking cessation as well as diet and fitness regimens. Well known fitness examples include the Nintendo Wii Fit and the Nike Plus iPhone app.

The nonprofit Hopelab organization, which develops innovative solutions to improve the health and quality of life of teens, has created a small device that records their physical activity as they walk around with it. The user periodically plugs this device into a computer and based on their activity levels, provides points that they can spend on virtual or real-world goods.

Science

Teams of online gamers took only three weeks to decipher the molecular structure of a key retrovirus enzyme that had been baffling scientists for over a decade. The gamers achieved their discovery by playing Foldit, an online puzzle game that allows players to use various tools provided by the game, and to collaborate and compete in predicting the structure of protein molecules.

Social Media

Foursquare is a web-based mobile application that allows registered users to post their location ("check-in") at a particular venue and connect with friends. It follows some of the gamification attributes of scoring points and attaining levels.

Innovation and Problem Solving

Evoke is a World Bank developed social network-based game whose goal is to help empower people all around the world to come up with creative solutions to our most urgent social problems.

The game is based on a compelling narrative story that engages players and offers top rewards such as online mentorship programs with business leaders, seed funding for new ventures, and travel scholarships to share their vision for the future.

Education and Training

Several new approaches to training that incorporate gamification have recently appeared. Examples include Code academy and Code School where players can learn to code and are rewarded with points and badges. This differs from Game Based Learning (GBL), whereby the subject matter applications have well defined learning outcomes that is balanced with game play.

Business

Organizations have begun to incorporate gamification principles into their businesses to achieve basic goals. Simple examples are businesses offering awards like virtual badges to induce their employees to embrace corporate goals and increase productivity. Another example is Target (TGT) stores improving cashier checkout performance by monitoring how long it takes to complete a purchase transaction. The cashier receives a score each time they check out a customer providing feedback as to whether they are performing up to standards. Target indicates that through the subtle game feedback, it is partially changing their employees' behavior to optimize their checkout transaction rate. From an enterprise perspective, this data is also aggregated and provided to management. This scoring and rating is akin to what gamers would see in playing video games.

Retail

Noted electronics manufacturer, Samsung has created Samsung Nation, which is a social media-based loyalty program that lets users earn badges for such activities as writing product reviews, sharing information about products with friends, watching product videos and competing for rewards.

Government

The archives of the National Library of Finland combined Crowd Sourcing and gaming to complete the extremely dull task of digitizing documents. They took something that needed to be digitized and broke the scanned documents up into millions of pieces, which were seeded into a game called Mole Bridge. In the Digitalkoot site, the players read the images of the individual words in those document pieces and typed them into the game window. Each word that is typed in helps build a bridge in the game. This created data was combined by the backend application to create the new cohesive digitized document. Redundancy is built in to the system to weed out potential errors.

New business models are emerging as gamification is providing an effective means to engage people by taking advantage of a humans' predisposition to gaming and social media. Organizations are beginning to leverage gaming principles in both the consumer world and business workplace to increase public interest in a product or service, drive incentive and behavior management in the workplace, or to provide a new channel for innovation through external tasking and problem solving.

Conclusion: Call to Action

What should I (or my organization) do now?

Action is the foundational key to all success
—Pablo Picasso

I start with the premise that the function of leadership is to produce more leaders, not more followers.
—Ralph Nader

Leadership Styles, Which One Are You?

Understanding leadership styles requires more than knowing leadership personality traits, achievements, or whether they are 'transformational'. Modesto Maidique, a visiting professor at Harvard Business School defines a six-level typology of leadership. A review of her work provides an explanation of what organizations and employees can expect from each type of leader.

Here are her six main leadership styles:

Level One: Sociopath
The first level of leader is the one who literally serves no one: the sociopath. This is the person who eventually destroys pretty much everything: value, those who surround him, and himself. Luckily, these are few and far between. Adolf Hitler is the classic example.

Level Two: Opportunist
This is the person who serves only him or herself, often at the expense of others. They're generally after wealth and power, and don't care about much else. Bernie Madoff provides a good example.

Level Three: Chameleon
These are the so-called leaders who try to please everyone, all the time. Needless to say, it doesn't work out too well. It's hard to find well-known corporate examples of this type, because they don't tend to rise too far in organizations.

Level Four: Achiever
At level four, we start to find people whom we can at least refer to as 'leaders' with a straight face. Executive ranks are filled with Achievers: These folks are goal-oriented, motivated, and good at beating sales quotas and earning their accolades at merit-award dinners. Their focus on corporate goals, however, can mean that they fail to see the larger picture. Former Hewlett-Packard CEO Mark Hurd may be in this category: Sure, HP's stock price more than doubled during his tenure, but he did it by slashing research and development.

Level Five: Builder
The Builder serves not a goal but an institution. These are the leaders with a grand vision that doesn't get derailed by fluctuations in short-term profit or stock market valuations. These are leaders that infect others with their enthusiasm, energy and integrity.

Level Six: Transcendent
There aren't many of these. These are the leaders who look to benefit all of society: thank Nelson Mandela or Martin Luther King, Jr.

What type of leader are you, and what type of leader do you strive to be? How about your boss?

Are you prepared to lead? Survey finds most are not

You may think of being promoted as the reward for all your hard work, but is this also a case may wish you were better prepared. For a significant percentage of new managers being prepared to lead is an issue if a new CareerBuilder survey is to be believed. The nationwide poll of nearly 4,000 workers revealed that finally getting on to the next rung of the career ladder can cause some serious stress.

The survey revealed that more than a quarter (26 percent) of new managers felt under prepared for their new responsibilities and a whopping 58 percent reported receiving no management training. So what did these fledgling bosses struggle with the most? CareerBuilder outlines the most commonly reported trouble spots for managers:

- Dealing with issues between co-workers — 25 percent
- Motivating team members — 22 percent
- Performance reviews — 15 percent
- Finding the resources needed to support the team — 15 percent
- Creating career paths for my team — 12 percent

Of course this blog provides great information that can help get new leaders comfortable with their new role.

What are you doing to prepare for the demands of 21st Century Leadership?

Leadership under Pressure

What is it that makes a good leader under pressure? A more important question is can one learn the traits required to lead under pressure? New York Times business writer Paul Sullivan, author of Clutch: Why Some People Excel Under Pressure and Others Don't recounts a talk he gave at West Point on the subject.

All leaders under pressure display five traits, he said: focus, discipline, adaptability, being present, and fear and desire.

There are three things business leaders can learn that will help them be successful under pressure:

1. Focused on a goal: Everything they do prepares them for the pressure filled moment and they know the responsibilities and the risks. Do you know what your primary mission is at work?

2. Continuous improvement: They develop an organization that is continually striving to be better. When a mistake happens, they try not to let it happen a second time. Are you aligned with the right organization? Or if you're leading that organization, are you prepared to change things that aren't working, even if change could be hard or even a reversal of something you implemented?

3. Practice for success: They know they have to be able to perform a task perfectly under normal conditions before they can expect to do it in a stressful situation. Can you say the same thing? Are you able to do your job at a high level every day? If not, then you should not be surprised when you make the wrong decisions under pressure."

Will following this advice mean you can lead under pressure? Well, maybe not–some people are just hard-coded for success in tough situations. But working at focusing on the objective, adaptability to the environment and improvement of skills sure puts whatever natural abilities you have in the best position to succeed when the going gets tough.

Have you developed any traits that help you lead under pressure?

Becoming a Recognized Expert in Innovation

How do you get to be considered an innovation expert? It helps if you are a bestselling author who promotes their books and brand on national television, or a university professor who has studied their subject for decades. But there is another kind of expert. It can be a person who is well-known and respected within their industry, frequently delivering key notes at conferences and winning plum consulting gigs. Here are the following five things anyone can do to start developing a recognized brand.

1. Develop a relationship with reporters who cover your subject area. The key here is to get to know the people who write about your field. Read your industry trade journals, local business weekly, and the business section of your metro newspaper regularly, and you'll quickly figure out who those reporters are.

2. Pitch yourself as a speaker. Reach out to your local. Chamber of Commerce or regional trade association and offer to speak on a specific topic. It's not immodest to suggest yourself - their program committees are often interested in good speakers.

3. Align with a high-profile client. As the saying goes, you're known by the company you keep. That means if you have well-known clients or associations, be sure to use them.

4. Create your own content. There's no better way to showcase your expertise than creating content others can read, review, and learn from. A blog like this one requires an on-going commitment. If you don't feel you have the time (or energy), then write an occasional article for an in-house newsletter or trade association publication. Looking for an even quicker solution? Use Twitter to demonstrate your expertise with pithy insights and links to relevant articles in your field.

5. Teach. It doesn't require a doctorate - many colleges and universities are hungry for skilled professionals to teach adjunct courses. The experience will sharpen your knowledge, enhance your presentation skills, and provide you with an added dose of prestige in your industry.

Have you developed other ways that increase your brand recognition as an expert in innovation?

10 Things Good Leaders Do!!

I've had good and bad leaders influence my career. I've thought about all the qualities that make up a good leader, and while it's hard to always do them I've got the top ten. Everyone has different experiences so these are based on my own experiences, good and bad.

1. Treat employees the way they deserve to be treated. You always hear people say they deserve respect and to be treated as equals. Well, some may not want to hear this, but respect must be earned.

2. Inspire your people. Inspire people by sharing your passion for the business. By knowing just what to say and do at just the right time to take the edge off or turn a tough situation around. Genuine anecdotes help a lot. So does a good sense of humor.

3. Encourage employees to hone their natural abilities and challenge them to overcome their issues. That's called getting people to perform at their best.

4. Build team spirit. Great groups outperform great individuals. And great leaders build great teams.

5. Take the heat and share the praise. It takes courage to take the heat and humility to share the praise. That comes

naturally to great leaders; the rest of us have to pick it up as we go.

6. Delegate responsibility, not tasks. Every leader delegates, but the crappy ones think that means dumping tasks they hate on workers. Good leaders delegate responsibility and hold people accountable. That's fulfilling and fosters professional growth.

7. Tell it to people straight, even when it's bad news. One of the most important things any leader can do is to man up and tell it to people straight. No sugarcoating, especially when it's bad news or corrective feedback.

8. Manage up … effectively. Good leaders keep management off employee's backs. Most people don't get this, but the most important aspect of that is giving management what they need to do their jobs. That's what keeps management away.

9. Pay people what they're worth, not what you can get away with. What you lose in expense you gain back several-fold in performance.

10. Take the time to share your experiences and insights. Labels like mentor and coach are overused. Let's be specific here. People learn from those generous enough to share their experiences and insights. They don't need a best friend or a shoulder to cry on.

First Critical Steps

Adaptive Leaders Drive Innovation via Failure Forward

Innovative leaders know how to foster innovation and tackle tough problems in an increasingly complex economy. One key to success is to embrace trial and error, develop the courage to risk and know failure–and adapt from those failures with adjustments - Accept Risk of Failure.

Innovative leaders face some challenges in large organizations. Big companies offer an attractive machine for carrying out correct decisions, the power of a team all pulling in the same direction, and clear responsibilities producing a proper flow of information up and down the chain of command. But, every one of these assets can become a liability...the big picture can become a self-deluding propaganda poster, the unified team retreats into group think, and the chain of command becomes a hierarchy of wastebaskets, perfectly evolved to prevent feedback from reaching the top."

Adaptive and innovative leadership focuses on accepting and tolerating failure. Here are three tips toward adaptive and innovative leadership:

1. Try new things with the expectation that some experiments will fail.
2. Make failure survivable...because it will be common.
3. And make sure you know when you've failed. When you rationalize or delude yourself about your mistakes, you tend to compound them by making stupid decisions in an effort to deny the failure ever happened (this is why people lose money at casinos).

Have you embraced risk of failure and how has it helped you?

Great Leaders get a Second in Command

Every business leader, executive, indeed, every manager needs a right-hand, a designated back up or a second-in-command. There are lots of reasons for that:

- Someone in charge when you travel or are out for whatever reason

- Someone who complements your strengths and fills in weaknesses
- Doubles effectiveness for certain tasks / responsibilities
- It's always good to have a strong "bench"
- Reduces stress on the organization and improves its effectiveness
- Succession planning

A second-in-command can be the most important person in your organization. The rub is they're very hard to find. They're even harder to find when you're not looking. It's actually shocking how many key managers, executives, and business leaders don't get how important it is to have a backup.

Having a second-in-command improves the effectiveness of every organization and is well worth the cost. Every key manager or leader should have one. As for finding that unique individual, it's just like a specialized executive search. Here are five tips useful in finding your second in command:

1. Know what you're looking for. First, you need to decide if you're truly trying to find a clone of yourself or someone who complements your weaknesses. They're usually two completely different people and the direction you take depends on your priorities, goals, and specific situation.

2. Know where to look. No, this is not obvious. There are times when you want to cultivate someone from within your organization or elsewhere in the company. Other times it's better to bring in a fresh perspective from outside.

3. You get what you pay for. This is a hire you don't want to skimp on. If you do, you run the risk of investing precious time and resources in someone who isn't going to cut it. In the long run, you stand to lose far more than you might save from cutting corners. Either hire someone who can substitute for you or don't. But don't do it halfway.

4. Look. Most managers don't have right-hand people because they're not looking. They don't see the value, it's not a priority, or they have some macho iron man thing going on. Well, there is tremendous value. It'll never be a priority until you really need someone and then you'll be in panic mode - not a good thing.

5. Motivate. Once they are on board, make sure they are motivated, engaged, and challenged. Some executives are coy about identifying their second-in-command. Don't be. If you have a back up, make sure they have authority and everyone knows it.

How are you working to identify your second in command?

Innovative Thinking- The Process and Tools

To reap the benefits of innovative thinking and apply it to a business problem, start by asking four strategic questions, what is, what if, what wows, and what works? Essentially, these are translated as:

- Assess the marketplace, get close to consumers to understand their behavior, talk to users

- Brainstorm and write down hypotheses; dream up your optimal, best-case-ever outcomes to a challenge; set aside constraints and fears to loosen up creativity;

- Cull options down to a manageable number that will "wow" the customer, combining upside value while presenting profit potential;

- Go into the marketplace with options and test the solution, product, or service with consumers, invite customers to co-create, and integrate feedback.

I've developed a number of tools to flesh out the answers to these four key process questions. Try using these four tools as part of your innovation process:

- Visualization: Use sketches, photographs, and other images to visualize a problem. Other techniques are storyboards that lay out a sequence of events with simple pictures, and creating fictional personas that visualize and represent typical customers.

- Customer journey mapping: A customer journey map means you "staple yourself to a customer" to empathize with a customer's experience from beginning to end with your brand. A book publisher could map a reader's journey, beginning with reading about a book online and in a review, through further research, deciding whether to purchase a print or e-book, where to purchase it, the reading experience, and what happened when they finished the book (email the author, post Amazon review).

- Assumption testing: Isolate and test key assumptions that will determine success or failure using thought experiments and simulations as you prepare to launch your solution or product. What assumptions are you making about your customers that need to be examined? Are you making assumptions regarding operational capacity? Assumptions about how your competitors will react?

- Customer co-creation: Engage the customer in the development of new business offerings. By putting prototypes in front of customers, you observe how they react, and integrate their responses to improve and change your offering. Often we get anxious about showing customers unfinished, unpolished stuff. Get over it. Innovation is about learning, and customers have the most to teach you.

Other tools include value chain analysis, mind mapping, brainstorming, rapid prototyping, and the learning launch.

Have you used visualization and other forms of innovative thinking to solve problems at work? What works for you and what doesn't?

The only source of profit, the only reason to invest in companies in the future is their ability to innovate and their ability to differentiate —Jeffery Immelt

The business climate continues to get tougher, more competitive, more accelerated in terms of change, and more challenging. Adapting to change poses a major impediment to achieving market leadership and competitive differentiation, as well as to ensuring survival. The emergence of an "always on" connected world has brought about a collapse of distance and time as the speed of information exchange has increased worldwide. This collapse is evidenced by the widespread reduction in product life cycles, the reduction in the duration of sustainable differentiation, the increase in competition and the blurring of business boundaries across all industries. The greater information exchange also increases the knowledge, expectations and choices of buyers, thereby tipping the traditional balance of power. The increased power of buyers has forced changes in the cost and pricing models of manufacturers' products. Manufacturers or service providers that formerly passed their costs on to buyers are now forced to lower their production or provision costs to make their products and services attractive to buyers. Buying power is reducing the overall profitability of industries.

As a result of these and other forces, lower profits and rapid change are structural realities for business, exposing weaknesses in every part of the organization: policy, strategy, operations, relationships and infrastructure. Changes in the business environment are outpacing the time it takes an organization to respond. An enterprise that cannot effectively reduce the time required to respond to change invites competitors to grab market share, supersede its position and even unravel its survival in the market. All these factors have narrowed the window of opportunity for businesses and are demanding new rules for recognizing opportunities and reacting effectively. Organizations need new ways to identify change and to respond quickly. They are being drawn to a new goal for agility: the ability of an organization to sense environmental change and respond efficiently and effectively to that change.

To navigate effectively through the dynamic market conditions that have given rise to the new focus on agility, organizations often must make major business transformations, change business direction, re-engineer business processes, and accelerate performance and execution.

David Gergen, author of *Eyewitness to Power: The Essence of Leadership Nixon to Clinton*, a superb study of presidential power, is correct in saying that the measure of a leader is the willingness to confront problems and seek solutions. That comes down to two factors that are essential to leadership success:

The commitment to action: Action begins with the decision to address a serious issue. You know the issue is a big problem when it has the potential to wreck your business, or alternately, when few people are willing to tackle the issue for fear it will wreck their careers.

The strength to follow through: Courage plays a part in this because it takes guts to stand up for what you believe, especially when your views are contrary to those in charge.

How well a leader exerts will and follows through with fortitude will shape that leader's legacy. We remember leaders for what they have accomplished rather than what they have avoided.

Addressing the tough issues may be the stuff of history but it is not something can be left to the books; it must be practiced every day. What factors are influencing your leadership approach? What have you identified, as must have leadership factors?

Acknowledgements

Leadership and Innovation, Harnessing New Forces Used by Business to Succeed grew from a number of learning experiences and activities that came together at just the right time.

As Senior Fellow and Chief Strategist at Lockheed Martin I became more aware of the responsibility and impact and solid and innovative leader can have on an individual and organization. In developing a personalized leadership plan I learn from some important experiences, i.e. development of a strategic plan for cloud computing, mentoring and coaching of Fellow candidates and teaching advanced studies and universities. These experiences put me in touch with leaders like Dr. Ray Johnson, Lockheed Martin CTO and others that demonstrated the value in developing a leadership mindset focused on monetizing the good ideas that we are often presented with.

I also lead a team of high potentials in the development of a detailed strategy for the application of advanced technologies (Cloud computing, Mobility, Big Data, Social Business) to core mission objectives of Government. This team is highly motivated and helped to shape my thoughts around how leadership should be developed and how innovation metrics should influence strategic planning and business transformation. One member of my team John Magnuson participated heavily in the development and review of this material and I'm thankful for his input. I learned to develop an easy to understand logic around the topics and developed much of the Reading Guide of my interactions with this team.

In developing the submission package for the BEYA Outstanding Technical Contribution Award, I was tasked with documenting my personal history. As I noted the educators, coaches and mentors that influenced me, it became clear that my mother was the most powerful and influential innovative leader that I had ever been exposed to. I decided to spend more time with her so she could help me decipher in more detail the complex relationship between leadership and innovation. I'm very thankful to Eleanor Dee for her love, guidance and wisdom. I've come to understand that the application of these important principles extends beyond the workplace and into your personal belief system. They drive your priorities and shape your life experiences. I pray that you find someone that can help you achieve the same outcome.

I truly want to thank my wife for her caring and support. As an author herself she has a unique understanding of what is required to organize, write edit and publish a book. Leadership and Innovation, Harnessing the New Forces Used by Business to Succeed would not exist without her.

Works Cited

(n.d.). Retrieved from businessdictionary.com: http://www. businessdictionary.com/definition/operational-effectiveness.html#ixzz2RsTnjoqz

(n.d.). Retrieved from mobile area education foundation: http:// maef.net

The innovation through acquisition strategy: Why the payoff iisn't always there. (2005, November 26). Retrieved from upenn.edu: http://knowledge.wharton.upenn.edu/article. cfm?articleid=1311

The bottom line: corporate performance and women's representation on boards. (2007, October 15). Retrieved from catalyst.org: http://www.catalyst.org/knowledge/ bottom-line-corporate-performance-and-womens-representation-boards

Connecting People to What Matters. (2008). Retrieved from www.Deloitte.com: http://www.deloitte.com/assets/ Dcom-UnitedKingdom/Local%20Assets/Documents/ UK_C_ConnectingPeopletoWhatMatters.pdf

Critical Path Initiative. (2009, April). Retrieved from Food and Drug Administration: http://www.fda.gov/ downloads/ ScienceResearch/SpecialTopics/CriticalPathInitiative/ UCM186110.pdf;

(2010). Retrieved from emcarts.org: http://www.emcarts.org/site/ emc_arts/assets/pdf/aif_innovation_rubric_overview.pdf

CMU Collective Intelligence Study. (2010, Oct). Retrieved from CMU News: http://www.cmu.edu/news/archive/2010/ October/oct1_collectiveintelligencestudy.shtml

Data, Data, Everywhere. (2010, February). Retrieved from http://www.economist.com/node/15557443

Innovation Leadership Requirements – Creativity. (2010, May 27). Retrieved from Innovation Excellence: http://www.businessweek.com/ innovate/content/may2010/id20100517_190221. htm?campaign_id=innovation_related

Remarks by the President on the "Educate to Innovate" Campaign. (2010, January 6). Retrieved from Whitehouse.gov: http:// www.whitehouse.gov/the-press-office/ remarks-president-education-innovate-campaign

Rising above the Gathering Storm, Revisited. (2010). Retrieved from bradley.edu: http://www.bradley.edu/ dotAsset/187205.pdf

The Rise of the Networked Enterprised - Web 2.0 finds its Payday. (2010, December). Retrieved from McKinsey & Co: http://www.mckinsey.com/insights/ high_tech_telecoms_internet/ the_rise_of_the_networked_enterprise_web_20 _finds_its_payday

What Chief Executives Really Want. (2010, May 18). Retrieved from Business Week: http://www.businessweek.com/ innovate/content/may2010/id20100517_190221. htm?campaign_id=innovation_related

Big Data: The next frontier for innovation, competition and productivity. (2011, May). Retrieved from http:// www.mckinsey.com/insights/business_technology/ big_data_the_next_frontier_for_innovation

Gartner Gamification Study. (2011, April 12). Retrieved from www.gartner.com: http://www.gartner.com/it/page. jsp?id=1629214

Jeff Bezos on Innovation. (2011, June 7). Retrieved from Geekwire: http://www.geekwire.com/2011/amazons-bezos-innovation/

the nist definition of cloud computing. (2011, March). Retrieved from cio research center: http://cioresearchcenter.com/2011/03/the-nist-definition-of-cloud-computing/

tns technology blog. (2011). Retrieved from tnsglobal.com: http://blogs.tnsglobal.com/tns_technology_blog/2011/06/did-you-know-that-globally-people-spend-3000000000-hours-a-week-playing-games-online-.html

(2012, February). Retrieved from howmanyarethere.org: http://www.howmanyarethere.org/how-many-mobile-phone-users-in-the-world/

Amazon's Jeff Bezos: The ultimate disrupter. (2012, November 16). Retrieved from CNN Money: http://management.fortune.cnn.com/2012/11/16/jeff-bezos-amazon/

2012 Businessperson of the Year. (n.d.). Retrieved from CNN Money: http://money.cnn.com/gallery/news/companies/2012/11/16/business-person-of-the-year.fortune/2.html

GE Healthcare Launches Social Media Driven Cancer Awareness and Prevention Campaign . (2012, August 20). Retrieved from Business Wire: http://www.businesswire.com/news/home/20120820005560/en/GE-Healthcare-Launches-Social-Media-Driven-Cancer

how many internet users are there in the world 2012. (2012). Retrieved from howmanyarethere.org: http://www.howmanyarethere.org/how-many-internet-users-are-there-in-the-world-2012/

Innovation Leadership Study. (2012, March). Retrieved from capgemini-consulting: http://www.capgemini-consulting.com/ebook/Innovation-Leadership-Study/index.html

Leading Through Connections CEO Case Study. (2012). Retrieved from ibm.com: http://public.dhe.ibm.com/common/ssi/ecm/en/gbe03485usen/GBE03485USEN.PDF

Social Media is reinvesnting how business is done. (2012, May). Retrieved from USA Today: http://usatoday30.usatoday.com/money/economy/story/2012-05-14/social-media-economy-companies/55029088/1

Social Media Report 2012. (2012, Dec). Retrieved from nielsen.com: http://www.nielsen.com/us/en/newswire/2012/social-media-report-2012-social-media-comes-of-age.html

Talent Tensions Ahead: A CEO Briefing. (2012, November). Retrieved from mckinsey.com: http://www.mckinsey.com/insights/economic_studies/talent_tensions_ahead_a_ceo_briefing

The World's Most Innovative Companies. (2012, September 5). Retrieved from Forbes: http://www.forbes.com/innovative-companies/

(2013). Retrieved from USAScienceFestival.org: www.USAScienceFestival.org

(2013, July 1). Retrieved from www.reuters.com: http://www.reuters.com/article/2013/07/01/il-ge-idUSnBw016065a+100+BSW20130701

(2013). Retrieved from global innovation index: http://www.globalinnovationindex.org/content.aspx?page=gii-full-report-2013#pdfopener

Apples acquisition strategy. (2013, February 22). Retrieved from techcrunch.com: http://techcrunch.com/2013/02/12/apples-acquisition-strategy-is-about-finding-great-talent-putting-it-to-work-on-existing-apple-priorities/

General Electric to realize benefits from social media data visualization software. (2013, January 29). Retrieved from Active Reports Server: http://www.activereportsserver.com/business-intelligence-news/

general-electric-to-realize-benefits-from-social-media-
data-visualization-software

How much to Americans know about Science. (2013, May).
Retrieved from Smithsonian Magazine: http://www.
smithsonianmag.com/ideas-innovations/How-Much-Do-
Americans-Know-About-Science.html#ixzz2RaG6dAF0

HR Disciplines. (2013, February). Retrieved from Society for
Human Resource Management: http://www.shrm.
org/hrdisciplines/staffingmanagement/Articles/Pages/
Improving-Talent-Management-Strategies.aspx

IFI Claims Patent Services. (2013, Jan). Retrieved from http://
ificlaims.com/index.php?page=news&type=view&id=ifi-
claims%2Fifi-claims-announces_2

MIT Computer Science and Artificial Intelligence Lab. (2013).
Retrieved from csail.mit.edu: http://www.csail.mit.edu/
events/eventcalendar/calendar.php?show=event&id=3535

NASA news releases. (2013, June 18). Retrieved from nasa.gov:
http://www.nasa.gov/home/hqnews/2013/jun/HQ_13-
188_Asteroid_Grand_Challenge.html

The world's 50 most innovative companies. (2013). Retrieved
from fastcompany.com: http://www.fastcompany.com/
most-innovative-companies/2012/full-list

Abhishek Kathuria, A. F. (2011, February 16). *Knowledge
Matters but culture is king (in technology acquisitions)*.
Retrieved from ssrn.com: http://papers.ssrn.com/sol3/
papers.cfm?abstract_id=1626330

Adner, R. (2012). *The Wide Lens: A New Strategy for
Innovation*. Portfolio Hardcover.

Alter, A. (2005, August 5). *Knowledge Workers need
better Insight*. Retrieved from CIO Insight:
http://www.cioinsight.com/c/a/Expert-Voices/
Knowledge-Workers-Need-Better-Management/

answers.com/topic/corporate-culture. (n.d.). Retrieved
from answers.com: http://www.answers.com/topic/
corporate-culture#ixzz2VpQ4A86M

Ashkenas, e. (2002). *The Boundaryless Organization: Breaking
the Chains of Organizational Structure.* Joissy-Bass.

Augustine, N. (2013). Retrieved from americansecurityproject.
org: http://americansecurityproject.org/blog/2013/
interview-norm-augustine-willpower-patience-needed-to-
improve-american-competitiveness/

Belleghem, S. V. (n.d.). *Getting ready for marketing 2020.*
Retrieved from sllideshare.net: http://www.slideshare.net/
stevenvanbelleghem

Benderly, B. L. (2010, February 22). *Does the US Produce Too
Many Scientists.* Retrieved from scientificamerican.
com: http://www.scientificamerican.com/article.
cfm?id=does-the-us-produce-too-m

Bennis, W. (2009). *On Becoming a Leader.* Basic Books.

Bidwell, M. (2012, March 28). *Why External Hires Get Paid
More, and Perform Worse, than Internal Staff.* Retrieved
from upenn.edu: http://knowledge.wharton.upenn.edu/
article.cfm?articleid=2961

Boris Groysberg, K. K. (2013). *The New Path to the C-Suite.*
Harvard Business Press.

Bouck, C. (2013). *The Lens of Leadership.* Avivia Publishing.

business dictionary/definition. (n.d.). Retrieved from
businessdictionary.com: http://www.businessdictionary.
com/definition/invention.html#ixzz2VMpzu9Eg

business dictionary/definition. (n.d.). Retrieved from
businessdictionary.com: http://www.businessdictionary.
com/definition/innovation.html#ixzz2VMpiCkw1

business dictionary/definition. (n.d.). Retrieved
from businessdictionary.com: : http://www.
businessdictionary.com/definition/innovation-strategy.
html#ixzz2VMbMgDoF

Business Value definition. (n.d.). Retrieved from wikipedia: http://en.wikipedia.org/wiki/Business_value

Castells, M. (2001). *The Internet Galaxy.* New York: Oxford University Press.

Christensen, C. (2011). *The Innovator's Dilemma.* Harper Business.

Cisco. (2012). Retrieved from Cisco. (n.d.). Cisco Visual Networking Index: Global Mobile Data Traffic Forcast 2012-2017.: (Cisco http://www.cisco.com/en/US/solutions/collateral/ns341/ns525/ns537/ns705/ns827/white_paper_c11-520862.html

Clinton, B. (1996). Retrieved from quotations page: www.quotationpage.com/quote/31751.html

Davenport, T. H. (2005). *Thinking for a living: How to get better performance and results from knowledge workers.* Boston: Harvard Business Press.

definition/talent. (n.d.). Retrieved from businessdictionary.com: http://www.businessdictionary.com/definition/talent.html#ixzz2WZa2OPfu

definition/talent. (n.d.). Retrieved from businessdictionary.com: http://www.businessdictionary.com/definition/talent.html#ixzz2WZa2OPfu

Definitions / Accountability. (n.d.). Retrieved from Business Dictionary: http://www.businessdictionary.com/definition/accountability.html#ixzz2VuYNbC9Z

Denning, S. (2012, November 2). *steve denning.* Retrieved from forbes.com: http://www.forbes.com/sites/stevedenning/2012/02/10/is-radical-management-too-risky/

Don Mankin, S. C. (2004). *Business without Boundaries.* Jossey-Bass.

Doss, H. (2013, April 24). *forbes/sites/henrydoss.* Retrieved from www.forbes.com: http://

www.forbes.com/sites/henrydoss/2013/04/24/
an-innovation-leadership-revolution-is-brewing/

Drucker, P. (1993). *Concept of the Coproration*. Transaction Publishers, Reprint edition.

Duhigg, C. (2012, February 16). *new york times magazine*. Retrieved from nytimes.com: : http://www.nytimes. com/2012/02/19/magazine/shopping-habits. html?pagewanted=all

email usage. (n.d.). Retrieved from trendingdig: http:// trendingdig.com/facts-about-email-usage-worldwide/

Engelmeier, S. (2012). *Inclusion: The New Business Advantage*. InclusionINC Media.

Esty, K. (1997). *Workplace Diversity: A Manager's Guide to Solving Problems and Turning Diversity into a Competitive Advanctage*. Adams Media Corporation.

Evangelista, B. (2011, July 18). *Netflix tried to ride out wave of customer anger*. Retrieved from San Fransisco Cronicle: http://www.sfgate.com/business/article/Netflix-tries-to-ride-out-wave-of-customer-anger-2354132.php 2011

Executive Sentiment Survey. (n.d.). Retrieved from Insigniam: http://insigniam.com/executive-sentiment-survey/

Fischetti, M. (2012, January). *How to make science and tech jobs more enticing to undergrads*. Retrieved from scientificamerican: http://www.scientificamerican.com/ article.cfm?id=graphic-science-science-tech-jobs-enticing

forbes leadership forum. (n.d.). Retrieved from www.forbes. com: http://www.forbes.com/sites/forbesleadershipfo rum/2012/05/30/10-commandments-for-delivering-bad-news/

From Overload to Impact: An Industry Scorecard on Big Data Business Challenges. (n.d.). Retrieved from oracle: http:// www.oracle.com/webapps/dialogue/ns/dlgwelcome. jsp?p_ext=Y&p_dlg_id=12350238&src=7546261&Act=4

Gartner IT Glossary. (n.d.). Retrieved from Gartner Group: http://www.gartner.com/it-glossary/service-oriented-architecture-soa/

Gladwell, M. (2007). *Blink: THe Power of Thinking without Thinking*. Back Bay Books.

Grance, P. M. (2011). *The NIST Definition of Cloud Computing*. Retrieved from http://csrc.nist.gov: http://csrc.nist.gov/publications/nistpubs/800-145/SP800-145.pdf

Hammer, M. (2003). *The Agenda: What every Business Must Do to Dominate the Decade*. Three Rivers Press.

Hartog, D. J. (2007). *How Leaders Influence Employees' Innovative Behaviour*. Retrieved from EmeraldInsight. com: http://www.emeraldinsight.com/journals. htm?articleid=1589092&show=html

Harvey Nash CIO Survey 2013. (n.d.). Retrieved from HarveyNash.com: http://media.harveynash.com/usa/mediacenter/HNash_CIO_Survey13-US.pdf

Hogg, M. (n.d.). *Intergroup leadership: a unifying force*. Retrieved from insead.edu: http://knowledge.insead. edu/leadership-management/talent-management/intergroup-leadership-a-unifying-force-2078

Holly, K. (n.d.). *usc.edu*. Retrieved from usc.edu: http://stevens.usc.edu/about_usc_stevens_team_krisztina_holly.php

Hughes, T. (2004). *American Genesis: A Century of Invention and Technological Enthusiasm, 1870-1970*. University of Chicago Press.

Ikujiro Nonaka, H. T. (1995). *The Knowledge Creating Company - How Japanese Companies Create the Dynamics of Innovation*. Oxford University Press.

incremental innovation. (n.d.). Retrieved from business dictionary: http://www.businessdictionary.com/definition/incremental-innovation.html#ixzz2ZIkGHeRh

Innovation by the Numbers. (n.d.). Retrieved from
www.innovation.org: http://www.innovation.
org/index.cfm/ToolsandResources/FactSheets/
Innovation_by_the_Numbers

innovation failure probable and costly. (n.d.). Retrieved
from the innovation and strategy blog: http://
theinnovationandstrategyblog.com/innovation/
innovation-challenges/innovation-failure-probable-and-
costly-12#sthash.FV9CeSmo.dpuf

innovation management. (n.d.). Retrieved from
innovation management: http://www.
innovationmanagement.se/2013/05/03/
what-is-innovation-governance-definition-and-scope/

intellectual property. (n.d.). Retrieved from business dictionary:
: http://www.businessdictionary.com/definition/
intellectual-property.html#ixzz2ZJTyG47x

James Collins, J. P. (1990). *Built to Last.* Harper Business.

Jane Stevenson, B. K. (2011). *Breaking Away: How Great
Leaders Create Innovation That Drives Sustainable
Growth – And Why Others Fail.* McGraw-Hill.

John Thill, C. B. (2004). *Excellence in Business
Communications.* Prentice Hall.

Johnson, M. (2010). *Seizing the White Space: Business Model
Innovation for Growth and Renewal.* Harvard Business
Press.

Johnson, S. (1998). *Who Moved My Cheese.* Penguin Group.

Labor, U. D. (2007, April). *The STEM Workforce Challenge.*
Retrieved from http://www.doleta.gov/youth_services/
pdf/STEM_Report_4%2007.pdf

Lopez, M. (2013, May 13). *GE Speaks on the Business Value
of the Internet of Things.* Retrieved from Forbes:
http://www.forbes.com/sites/maribellopez/2013/05/10/
ge-speaks-on-the-business-value-of-the-internet-of-things/

Luger, J. (2013, May). *Why Mobile Commerce is set to Explode.* Retrieved from www.businessinsider.com: http://www. businessinsider.com/why-mobile-commerce-is-set-to-explode-2013-5#ixzz2Tpts7Dbl

Malandro, L. (2009). *Fearless Leadership.* McGraw-Hill.

Mayer, M. (2009, August). Retrieved from Parc.com: http:// www.parc.com/event/936/innovation-at-google.html

McDonald, M. P. (2011, January 27). *Judgement Workers - the next step beyond Knowledge Workers.* Retrieved from Gartner: http://blogs.gartner.com/ mark_mcdonald/2011/06/27/judgment-workers-%E2%80%93-the-next-step-beyond-the-knowledge-worker/

McManus, R. (2010, May). *The Coming Data Explosion.* Retrieved from readwrite.com: http://readwrite. com/2010/05/30/the_coming_data_explosion

Metcalf, M. (n.d.). *innovative-leadership-workshop.* Retrieved from innovativeleadershipfieldbook.com: http:// www.innovativeleadershipfieldbook.com/book-series/ innovative-leadership-workbook-for-emerging-leaders/

Michaels, D. (2013, January 24). *innovation is messy business.* Retrieved from wall street journal: http://online.wsj.com/ article/SB10001424127887323301104578257862879948 292.html

Mika, S. (2007, January 11). *The Four Drivers of Innovation.* Retrieved from Gallup Business Journal: http:// businessjournal.gallup.com/content/26068/Four-Drivers-Innovation.aspx

Morton, P. (2013, May). *Strategies for a successful customer centric business model.* Retrieved from IBM Smarter Commerce blog: http://www.smartercommerceblog. com/commerce/2013/04/11/strategies-for-a-successful-customer-centric-business-model/

Murray, A. (2010). *The Wall Street Journal Essential Guide to Management*. Harper Business.

News, I. (2010, June). *ITU News*. Retrieved from http://www.itu.int/net/itunews/issues/2010/05/12.aspx

P&G Drives New Product Innovation to the Next Level with Increased Crowdsourcing Program. (n.d.). Retrieved from DailyCrowdsource.com: http://dailycrowdsource.com/20-resources/projects/203-pg-drives-new-product-innovation-to-the-next-level-with-increased-crowdsourcing-program

Pearson, B. (2012). *The Loyalty Leap: Turning Customer Information into Customer Intimacy*. Portfolio Hardcover.

philippe-deschamps, j. (2012, August). *governing innovation models*. Retrieved from imd: http://www.imd.org/research/challenges/governing-innovation-models-jean-philippe-deschamps.cfm

Porter, M. (1998). *Competetive Strategy*. Free Press.

Porter, M. E. (1998). *Competitive Strategy: Techniques for Analyzing Industries and Competitors* . Free Press.

Ready to Innovate. (n.d.). Retrieved from conference board: http://www.artsusa.org/pdf/information_services/research/policy_roundtable/readytoinnovatefull.pdf

Report, L. W. (2010). Retrieved from http://www.theleadershipcircle.com/flexability-agility-innovation

Schyns, B. (2010). *When Leadership Goes Wrong Destructive Leadership, Mistakes, and Ethical Failures*. Information Age Publishing.

Shalom Saar, M. H. (2012). *Leading with Conviction: Mastering the Nine Critical Pillars of Integrated Leadership*. Jossey-Bass.

Space technology spinoffs cellphone camera. (n.d.). Retrieved from Science.com: http://www.space.com/10635-space-spinoff-technology-cellphone-camera.html

Space technology spinoffs ultraviolet sunglasses. (n.d.). Retrieved from Space.com: http://www.space.com/11141-space-technology-spinoffs-ultraviolet-sunglasses.html

Stark, P. (n.d.). *What matters to employees.* Retrieved from peterstark.com: http://www.peterstark.com/2010/what-matters-to-employees/

Tellis, G. (2013). *Unrelenting Innovation: How to Build a Culture for Market Dominance.* Jossey-Bass.

The world's most innovative companies. (n.d.). Retrieved from cnn.com: http://money.cnn.com/magazines/fortune/mostadmired/2011/best_worst/best1.html

Thomas Cheesebro, L. O. (2006). *Communication Skills: Preparing for Career Success.* Prentice Hall.

Tom Rath, B. C. (2009). *Strengths based Leadership.* Gallup Press.

Union, I. T. (2012). *ITU Measuring the Information Society 2012 Report.* Retrieved from http://itu.int/ITU-D/ict/publications/idi/material/2012/MIS2012_highlights_short.pdf

Vijay Govindarajan, C. T. (2010). *The Other Side of Innovation.* Harvard Business Review Press.

What is Content Marketing? (n.d.). Retrieved from Content Marketing Institute: http://contentmarketinginstitute.com/what-is-content-marketing/

Wilson, M. (2007). *Closing the Leadership Gap.* Penguin Books; Revised edition.

Reading Group Guide

Critical thinking regarding leadership and innovation can be found from some great organizations and innovative leaders. Here are a few selected readings that will round out the many views on the subject.

1. *The Innovator's Solution: Creating and Sustaining Successful Growth – Clayton Christensen.* In The Innovator's Solution, Clayton Christensen and coauthor Michael E. Raynor build on Christensen's groundbreaking disruptive innovation research to help all companies understand how to become disruptors themselves. They not only reveal that innovation is more predictable than most managers have historically believed, but they also provide clear advice on the business decisions crucial to truly disruptive growth. Utilizing in-depth research of multiple companies and industries, the authors identify what actions and practices are essential for companies to embrace new disruptive innovations and avoid being disrupted themselves. The Innovator's Solution is an important addition to any innovation library.

2. *Innovation and Entrepreneurship – Peter F. Drucker.* The first book to present innovation and entrepreneurship as purposeful and systematic discipline, which explains and analyzes the challenges and opportunities of America's new entrepreneurial economy. A superbly practical book that explains what established businesses, public survey institutions, and new ventures have to know, have to learn, and have to do in today's economy and marketplace.

3. *Breaking Away: How Great Leaders Create Innovation that Drives Sustainable Growth--and Why Others Fail - Jane*

Stevenson, Bilal Kaafarani. Breaking Away provides the framework to be that leader—and to create other leaders who will drive your company into a future of profits and growth. Pioneers in the field of innovation leadership, Jane Stevenson and Bilal Kaafarani provide a simple but powerful model for breaking away from your industry pack by fully utilizing your employees, technology, and resources. You'll learn how: Ford beat Toyota in the race to create the first hybrid (and why everyone thinks it was vice versa) GE's development of a locomotive battery makes planet earth more sustainable Skype landed 480 million registered users in its first four years of business Emirates airline has grown from a small, regional carrier to one of the world's top three airlines Different organizations, different industries . . . one thing in common: a cadre of leaders who understand the nature of innovation, develop well-defined priorities, and maintain a powerful sense of accountability. Breaking Away will change the way you approach leadership and innovation—and put you on the road to market domination.

4. *The Transformational CIO: Leadership and Innovation Strategies for IT Executives in a Rapidly Changing World - Hunter Muller.* The Transformational CIO is chock full of stimulating thought leadership and useful knowledge that will help you leverage new and existing technologies to create business value, generate more revenue, increase profits and improve customer relationships in rapidly changing global markets. This book is a practical guide for senior executives seeking optimal returns on technology investments, now and in the future.

5. *Leadership and Innovation: Entrepreneurs in Government - Jameson W. Doig and Erwin C. Hargrove.* This book outlines a perspective on leadership in government that emphasizes entrepreneurship. They show how government executives' ability to set goals, generate support inside and

outside the bureaucracy, and implement innovative ideas--
even at risk to their own careers-- can have a significant
impact on their organizations and on society. Doig and
Hargrove describe their styles as ranging from "rhetorical
leaders" to "entrepreneurial administrators." Yet these
diverse leaders share some important traits, including a
capacity to see historical opportunity, the ability to mobilize
constituencies, and a desire to "make a difference."

6. Big Data Analytics: Disruptive Technologies for Changing
the Game - Arvind Sathi. Bringing a practitioner's view
to big data analytics, this work examines the drivers
behind big data, postulates a set of use cases, identifies
sets of solution components, and recommends various
implementation approaches. This work also addresses and
thoroughly answers key questions on this emerging topic,
including; what is big data and how is it being used? How
can strategic plans for big data analytics be generated? How
does big data change analytics architecture?

7. *The Innovator's Dilemma: When New Technologies
Cause Great Firms to Fail – Clayton Christensen.* Clayton
Christensen demonstrates how successful, outstanding
companies can do everything "right" and yet still lose
their market leadership – or even fail – as new, unexpected
competitors rise and take over the market. Through this
compelling multi-industry study, Christensen introduces his
seminal theory of "disruptive innovation" that has changed
the way managers and CEOs around the world think about
innovation. While decades of researchers have struggled to
understand why even the best companies almost inevitably
fail, Christensen shows how most companies miss out on
new waves of innovation. His answer is surprising and
almost paradoxical: it is actually the same practices that
lead the business to be successful in the first place that
eventually can also result in their eventual demise.

Questions and Topics for Discussion

Leaders struggle to inspire curiosity, challenge current perspectives in order to create the freedom to innovate. Here are some meaningful questions and topics for thought or discussion with your peers.

Compared to previous years is leadership changing, if so why?

The context for leadership has changed dramatically. Leading people and organizations is fundamentally more complicated today than it was even several years ago and is not getting any easier. Being agile in order to stay current with their business, as the pace of change has accelerated so dramatically. Consider what is driving the changes in leadership:

- Moving at Internet Time requires more rapid decision making
- Information overload from newly available information
- Innovative technologies that create new challenges
- Increased global and economic interactions, interconnections and uncertainties
- The new global and diverse workforce
- Dealing with employees who live with anxiety, who are stressed by over work and job security
- Maintaining and growing your client base
- Increasing budgetary constraints to do more with less
- New laws, rules and regulatory burdens

How would you address any of these areas within your organization?

Clearly, leading a business is becoming more complex and decision making more difficult. But the guiding principles, such as building good relationships, communicating well, and creating an environment of trust and respect, should remain the same.

Leadership soft skills will continue to play an increasingly important role as leaders need to do more with less.

Areas of change include:

- Understanding customers' current needs along while accurately predicting future needs as well.
- Improving social skills to deal with diversity and globalization
- The ability to inspire others counts more in managing complex environments.
- The need to innovate is being driven by the global economy.
- Employees need to have better information and be able to collaborate with their co-workers.
- Leaders need to push more decision-making down to the employee level

As a result, corporations require leaders who know how to handle themselves in this complex environment.

Is leadership driving innovation? If so how?

Surveys have shown that business leaders constantly confirm that innovation is among their priorities, they are generally disengaged in facilitating this across their organizations, regardless of size. Articles about the leadership gap in innovation continue to be topics of discussion in articles and seminars. Recently, the Information Technology Innovation Foundation ranked the U.S. last of 40 countries in terms of improved innovation capacity over the past decade. In the meantime, China's government investment in corporate innovation is expected shortly to outpace that of the

United States. So to answer the question "is leadership driving innovation", the answer is not well or not well enough. Yes, there are organizations such as Google, that are extremely innovated, from top-down, but as they grow in size, they too admit some difficulties in managing innovation.

According to the conclusions from a joint study by Capgemini Consulting and IESE in their report "Innovation leadership study", the most important constraint for companies to reach their innovation target is a "well-articulated innovation strategy". So regardless of the size of your organization, the question is, "do you have a well-documented strategy to deal with innovation?

One important aspect is hiring and retaining the right people. How do you attract experts to your team? How creative are your people? While engineers or IT personnel may be great at what they do, they may not have what it takes to transform creativity into valuable innovations.

Sun Microsystems founder Bill Joy stated, "Innovation happens elsewhere." He characterize it as meaning that whatever you are doing, and no matter how many smart people are on your team, there are always more smarter people elsewhere. So how can you leverage those people? If you're developing software, are there APIs or Open Source software that can enhance and differentiate your product?

How do you change company culture so that people are more likely to share ideas? How do you make cultures more open to embracing new ideas to create useful innovation for customers?

What is your organization doing to drive innovation?

What challenges are associated with leading with innovation in mind?

Innovation is a powerful concept that is often difficult for corporations, regardless of their size, to grasp. Companies tend to do things in the way that they always have because it works well for them. The first challenge is for a leader to overcome that inertia and lead with innovation in mind.

The stronger the culture of innovation is within the organization, the greater the likelihood of innovative behaviors. Sometimes organizations struggle with three well-known concepts that are commonly confused and misunderstood: vision, values and strategy. They are separate and distinct concepts, but when all three are used appropriately, they can keep your business on track. A great vision should provide the basis of inspiration to everyone in the organization and that vision needs to incorporate innovation. A vision must also be structurally sound and attainable. Vision may be modified over time to reflect changes in direction or as new opportunities present themselves to the organization.

The vision statement differs from the how the company intends to make that future into a reality, which is part of a mission statement.

A vision defines your business and what it stands for – not what it does. Values are sometimes referred to as the business culture and an organization needs to establish a culture of innovation. Ultimately, it's how you want the people who work there to interact with others in their daily work. Businesses typically describe their values by using words such as accountability, integrity, innovation, and teamwork. Values are a contributor to Vision. Whereas a vision can change over time, values should be a constant and are part of your business DNA.

Only after you've defined values and vision can you define how you're going to get there. While the vision articulates where we are going; the strategic plan tells us how we're actually going to get there.

Strategy is fluid can typically changes either incrementally or radically over time as business conditions, customer requirements and global competition are constantly in a state of flux.

The end aim is that so all those involved within the organization, or closely associated with it, can relate too and 'gather' around an overarching framework, articulated and constructed from the top, that guides innovation.

What values, vision, and strategies do you have for your company?

Once these are in place, leaders always find significant challenge in the commitment of the fundamental ingredients or resources of people, time, money that lets innovation flourish and grow. While good short-term reasons are often cited, it is still not an excuse in not attempting to plant the seeds of innovation.

Innovation equates to coming up with new ideas, which requires having the right mix of creative and motivated people as a part of your team that are positioned to move your innovation forward.

In the future what will results be from the relationship between leadership and innovation?

The link between leadership and innovation is clear today. Creative leaders will have to develop human capital, and strive to create and maintain an environment favorable for new idea creation and innovation within the organization. The first result is the ability to create a corporate culture and environment that fosters innovation is crucial. A transformational leader establishes that vision and associated strategy that is embedded in the DNA of the company. An innovation nurturing process throughout the organization can potentially grow new leaders. Leaders and their respective organizations need to walk the walk. To facilitate communications, leaders should also establish a framework for innovation whereby common practices and vocabularies are shared. Develop a form of idea management, whereby key leadership has greater involvement in idea creation.

As a leader, you need a strong skill set and operational plan that addresses current circumstances; but you must also cultivate a readiness to quickly change and adapt your thinking when it's not working. Innovative and creative thinking need the right combination of activity and reflection.

A leader supports teams and individuals as they turn their creative efforts into innovations. A leader also manages the organization's goals and activities aimed at innovation.

List of Acronyms

3-D	Three Dimensional
AOL	America On Line
API	Application Programming Interface
AR	Augmented Reality
AT&T	American Telephone & Telegraph
AWS	Amazon Web Services
BBC	British Broadcasting Company
BEYA	Black Engineer of the Year Award
BI	Business Intelligence
BPO	Business Process Outsourcing
BYOD	Bring Your Own Device
CapEx	Capital Expenditures
CeNSE	Central Nervous System for the Earth
CEO	Chief Executive Officer
CFO	Chief Financial Officer
CIO	Chief Information Officer
CLO	Chief Learning Officer
CMU	Carnegie Mellon University
CoSTEM	Council Committee on STEM Education
CPU	Central Processing Unit
CRM	Customer Relationship Management
CSA	Cloud Security Alliance
CSP	Cloud Service Provider
CSS	Cascading Style Sheet
CTO	Chief Talent Officer
CTO	Chief Technology Officer
CX	Customer Experience
DBMS	Data Base Management System
DIY	Do It Yourself
EDS	Electronic Data Systems

EOP	Executive Office of the President
GE	General Electric
EFT	Electronic Funds Transfer
ETL	Extract, Transform and Load
EYE	Engaging Youth through Engineering
FDA	Food and Drug Administration
FEAC	Federal Enterprise Architect Certification
GBL	Game Based Learning
GII	Global Innovation Index
GPS	Global Positioning System
GUI	Graphical User Interface
HBCU	Historically Black Colleges and Universities
HBS	Harvard Business School
HCI	Human Computer Interaction
HD	High Density
HIT	Human Intelligence Task
HP	Hewlett Packard
HR	Human Resources
HTML	Hyper Text Markup Language
IBM	International Business Machines
IESE	Instituto de Estudios Superiores de la Empresa (Business School)
IM	Instant Messaging
IOT	Internet of Things
IP	Intellectual Property
IT	Information Technology
JIT	Just In Time
JPL	Jet Propulsion Lab
LLC	Limited Liability Corporation
LIG	Leadership, Innovation and Growth
M2M	Machine-to-Machine
MIT	Massachusetts Institute of Technology
MMOG	Massively Multiplayer Online Games
MOOC	Massive Online Open Course
NASA	National Aeronautics and Space Administration
NCOIC	Network Centric Operations Industry Consortium

NGA	Northgate Arinso
NIH	Not Invented Here
NIST	National Institute of Standards and Technology
NOAA	National Oceanic and Atmospheric Administration
NSF	National Science Foundation
NSTC	National Science and Technology Council
OMB	Office of Management and Budget
OpEx	Operational Expenditures
OS	Operating System
OSS	Open Source Software
PARC	(Xerox) Palo Alto Research Center
PC	Personal Computer
PISA	Program for International Student Assessment
P&G	Proctor & Gamble
QS	Qualified Self
RIM	Research In Motion
ROI	Return on Investment
R&D	Research & Development
SaaS	Software as a Service
SHRM	Society for Human Resource Management
SOA	Service Oriented Architecture
SST	Super Sonic Transport
STEAM	Science Technology Engineering Art and Math
STEM	Science Technology Engineering and Math
TCO	Total Cost of Ownership
TCP/IP	Transmission Control Protocol / Internet Protocol
UNCF	United Negro College Fund
UX	User Experience
WIPO	World Intellectual Property Organization
WWW	World Wide Web
WYSIWYG	What You See Is What You Get

Index

About the Author

Melvin Greer is Senior Fellow and Chief Strategist, with over 25 years of systems and software engineering experience; he is a recognized expert in Service Oriented Architecture, Cloud Computing, Mobility, Big Data and Social Business. Mr. Greer has been awarded the BEYA 2012 Technologist of the Year Award, which recognizes his outstanding technical contribution and technical products that have a broad impact and high value to society as a whole. Mr. Greer has held numerous senior leadership positions, helping global enterprises based in Germany, U.K., and Brazil with their reengineering and transformational initiatives.

In addition to his professional and investment roles, he is the Founder and Chief Executive Officer of the Greer Institute for Leadership and Innovation, formed to apply Greer's research and to help find solutions to some of the most important global leadership and innovation challenges.

Mr. Greer is a frequent speaker at conferences and universities and is an accomplished author; "The Web Services and Service Oriented Architecture Revolution" and "Software as a Service Inflection Point, Using Cloud Computing to Achieve Business Agility" are his most recently published books.